Just Teacups

Advanced Coloring Book

This book belongs to

____

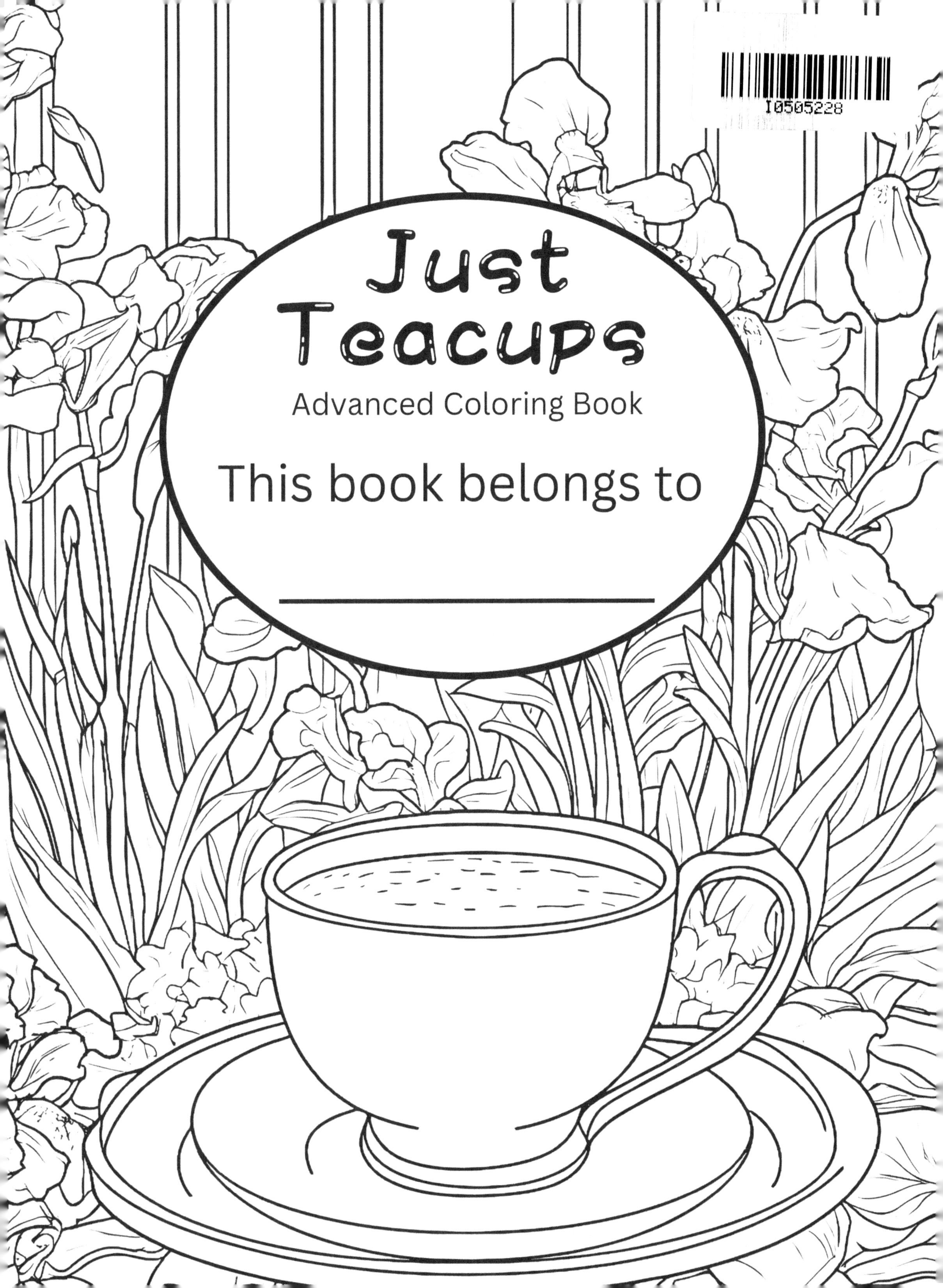

Whimsical Hues

Coloring books

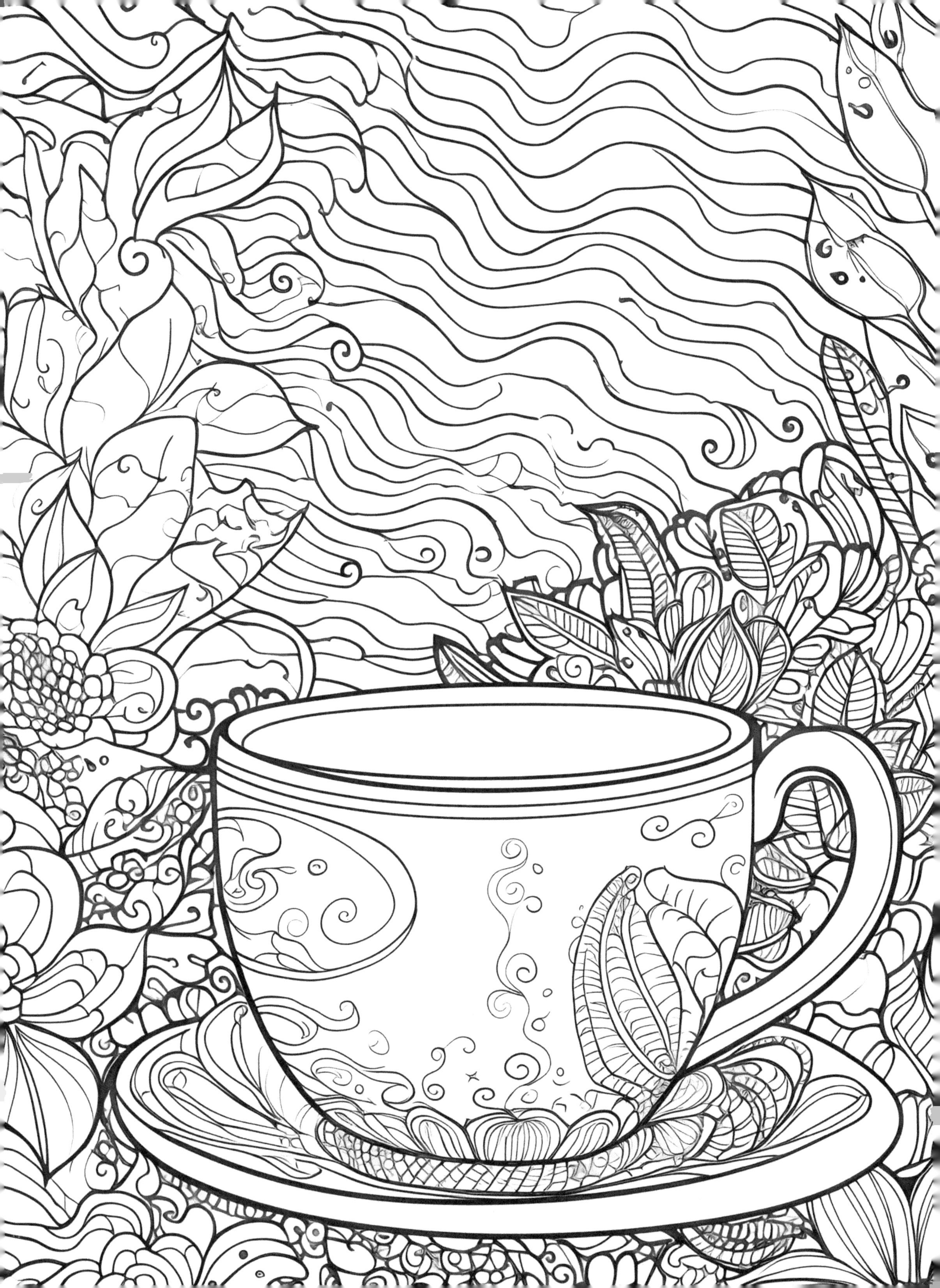

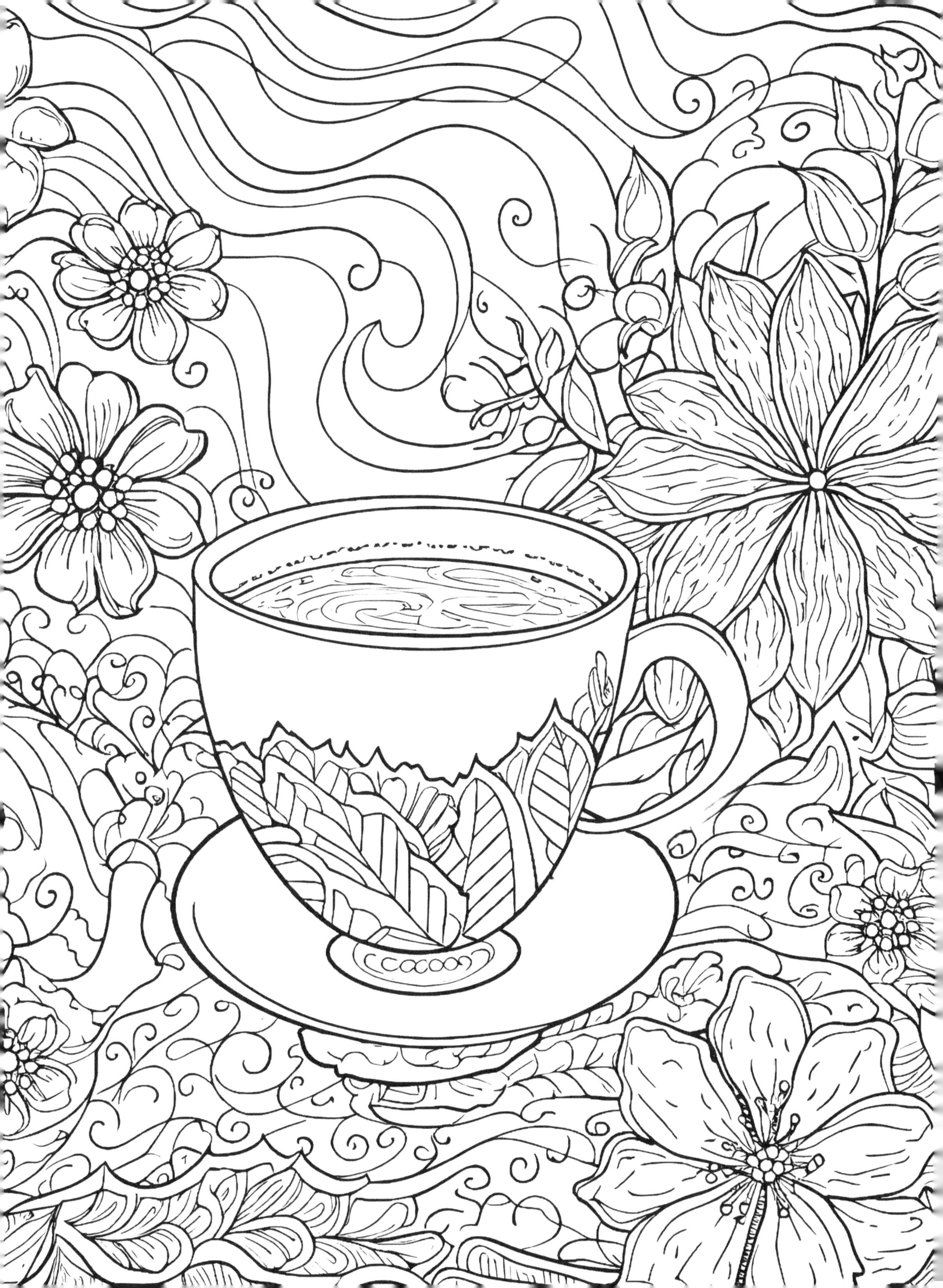

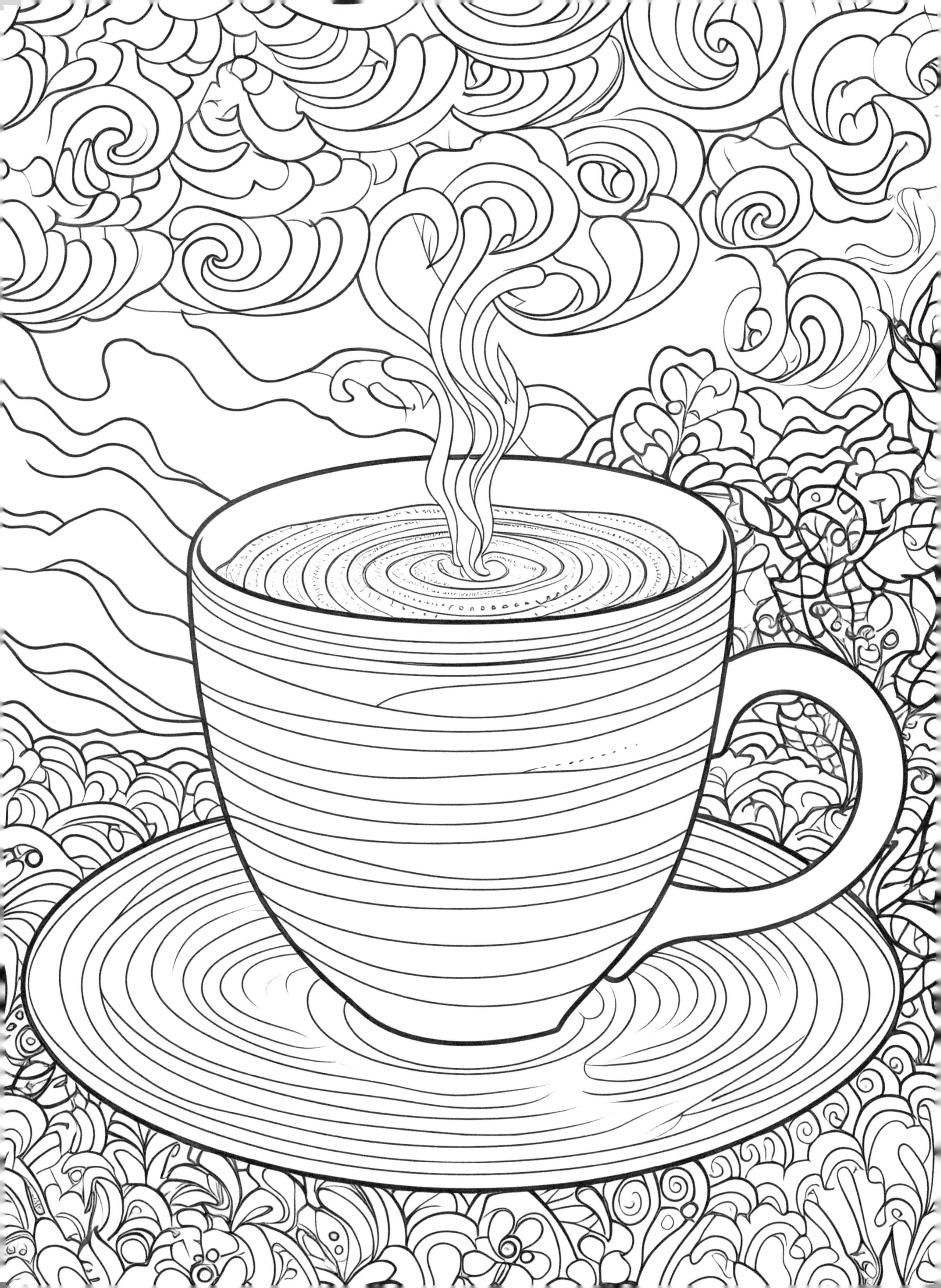

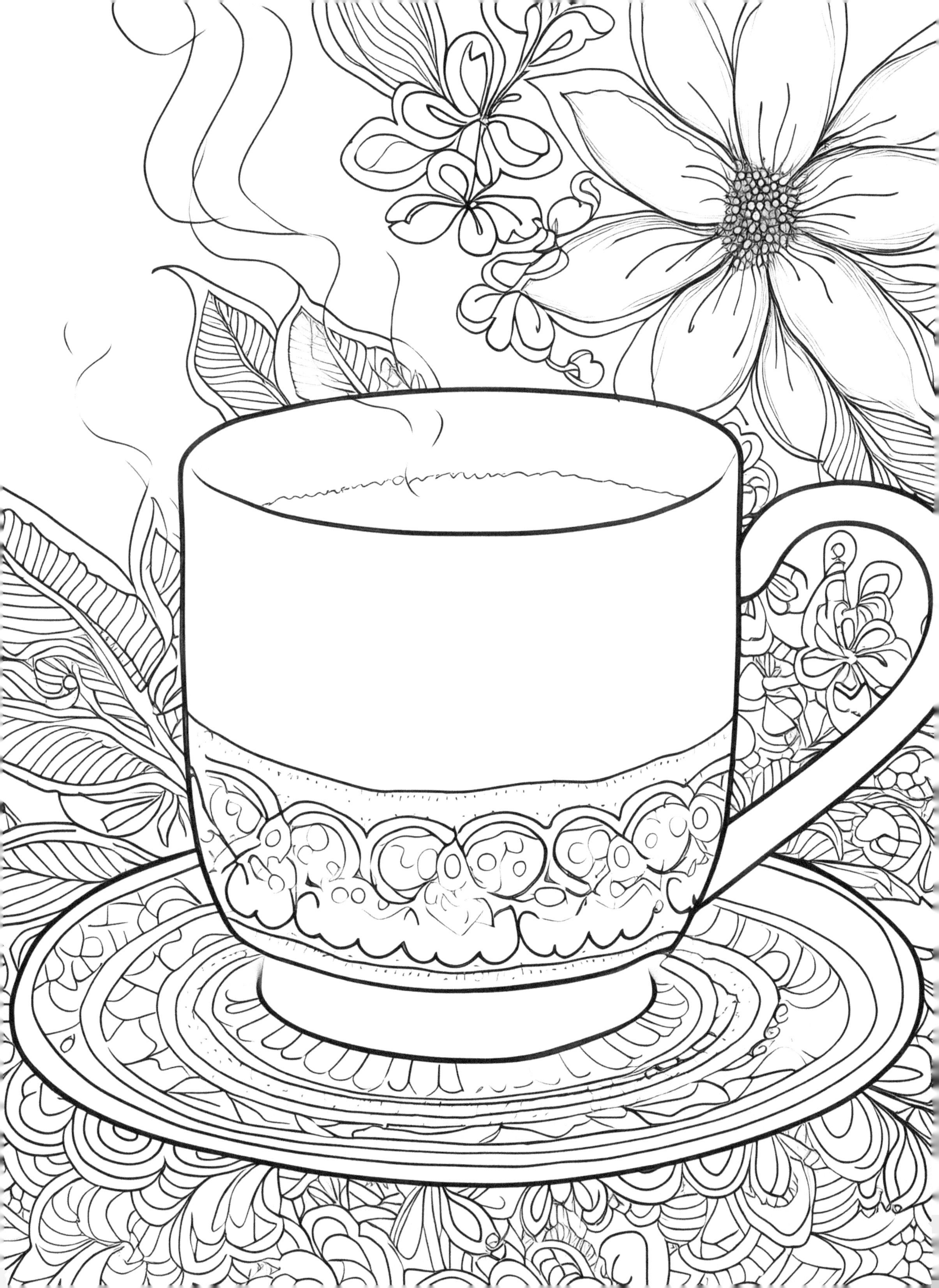

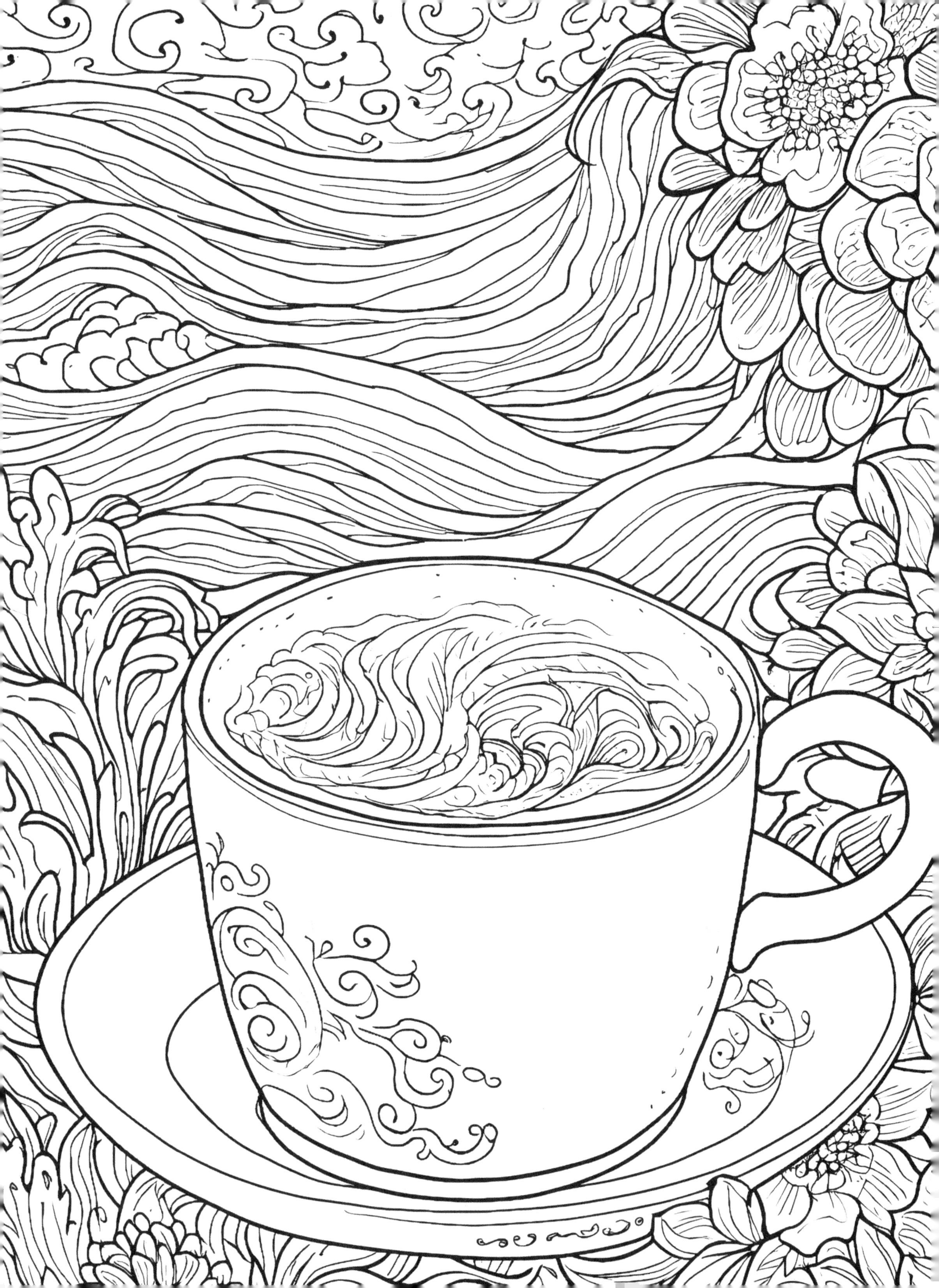

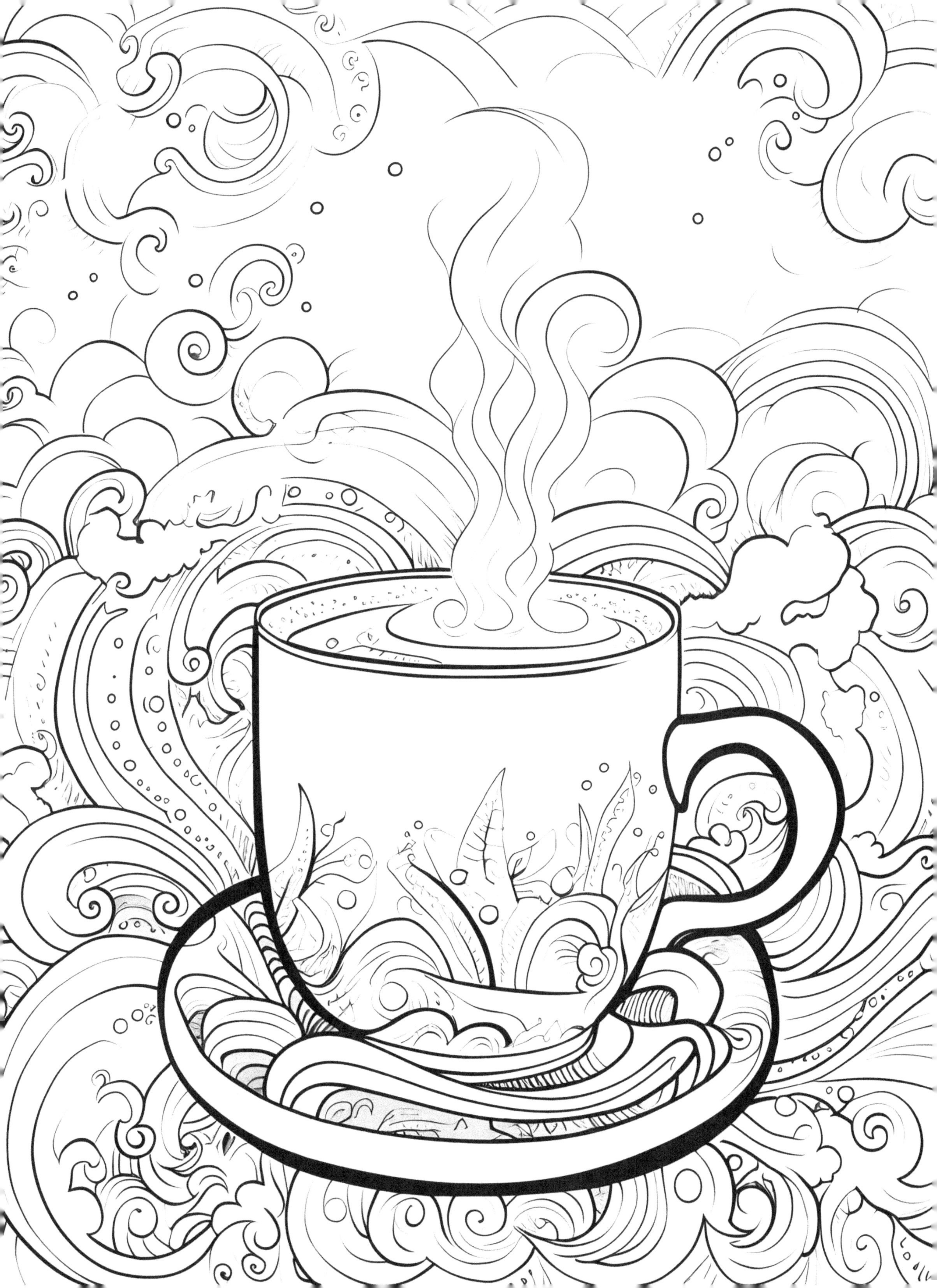

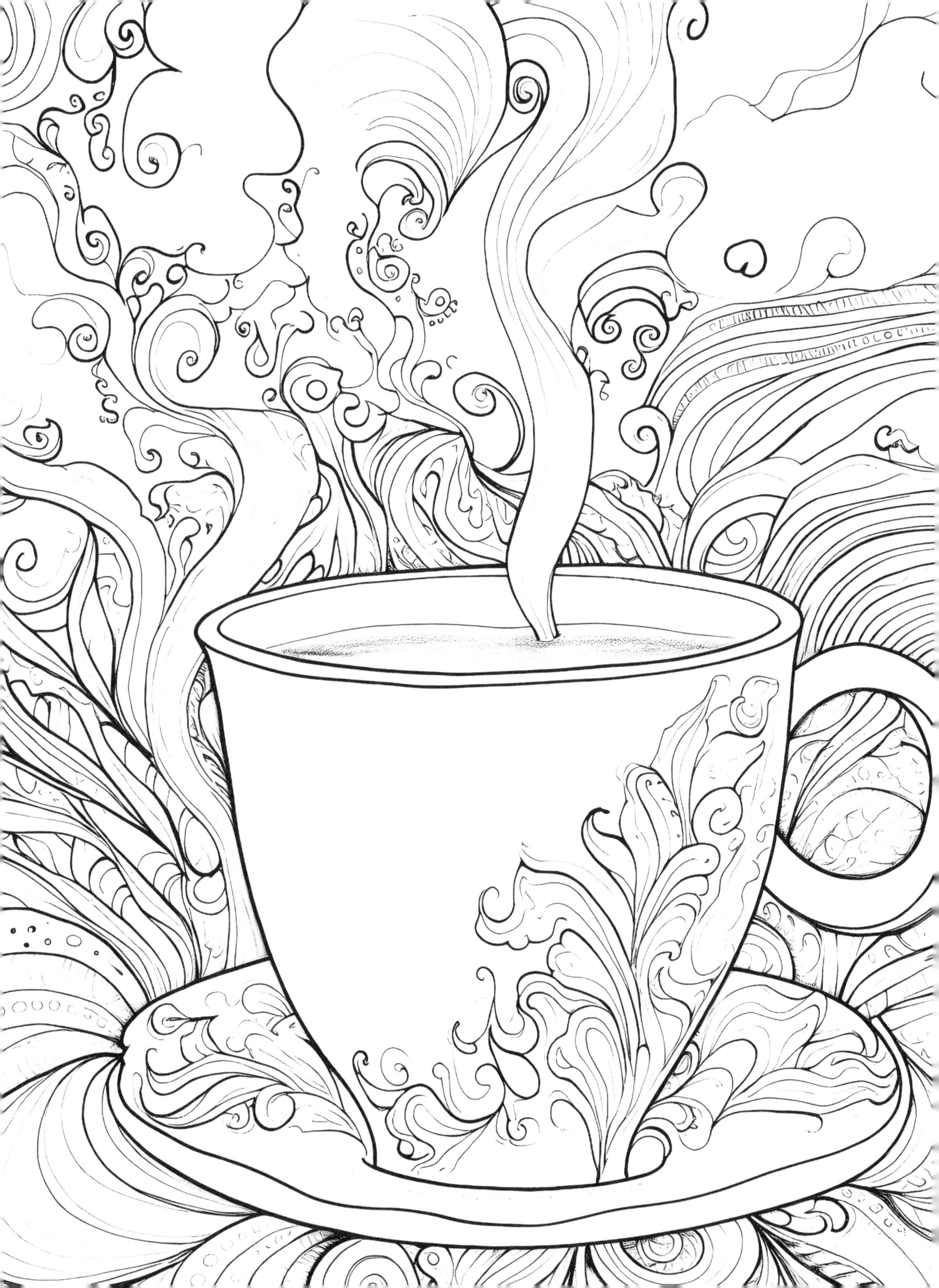

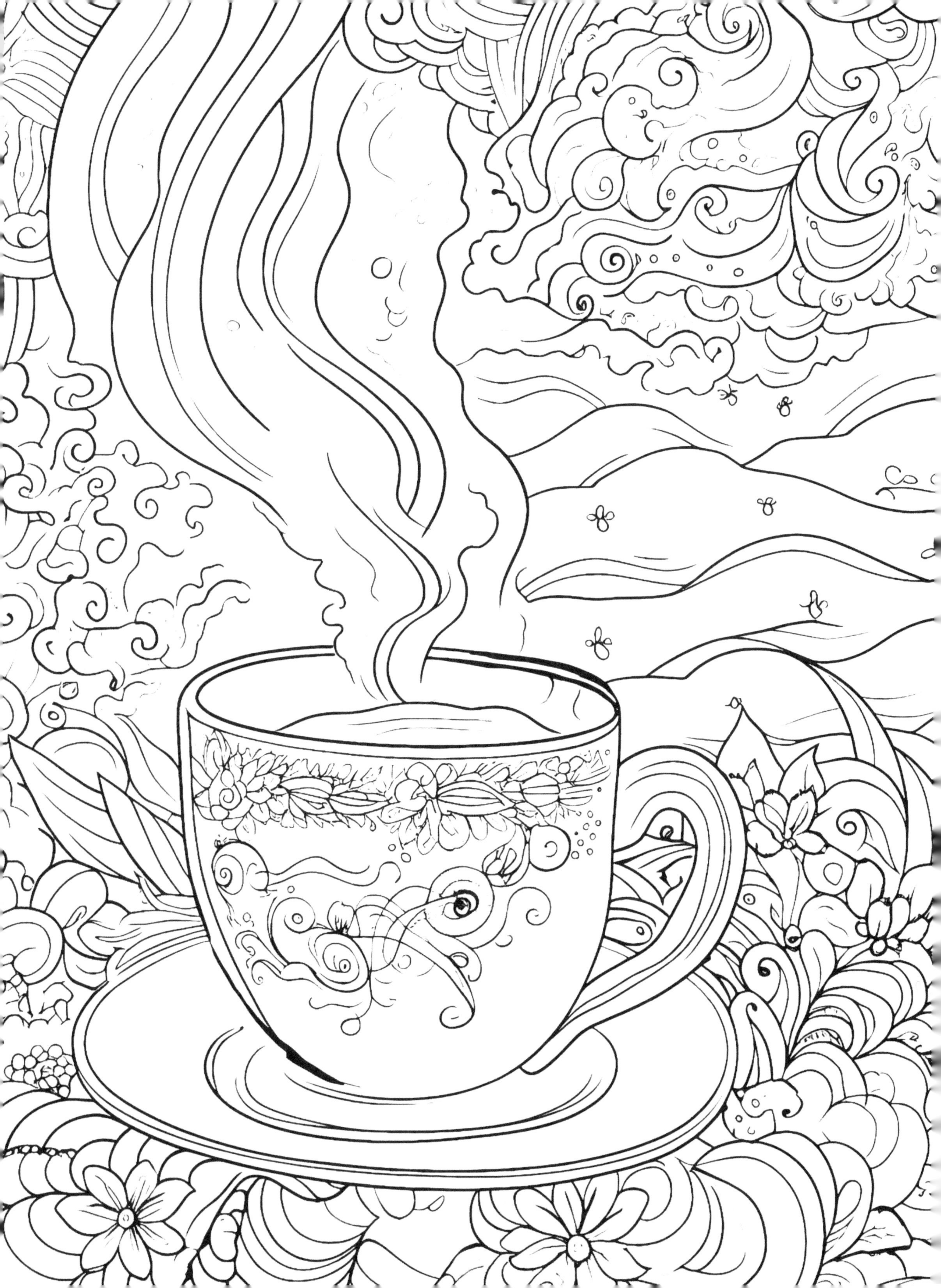

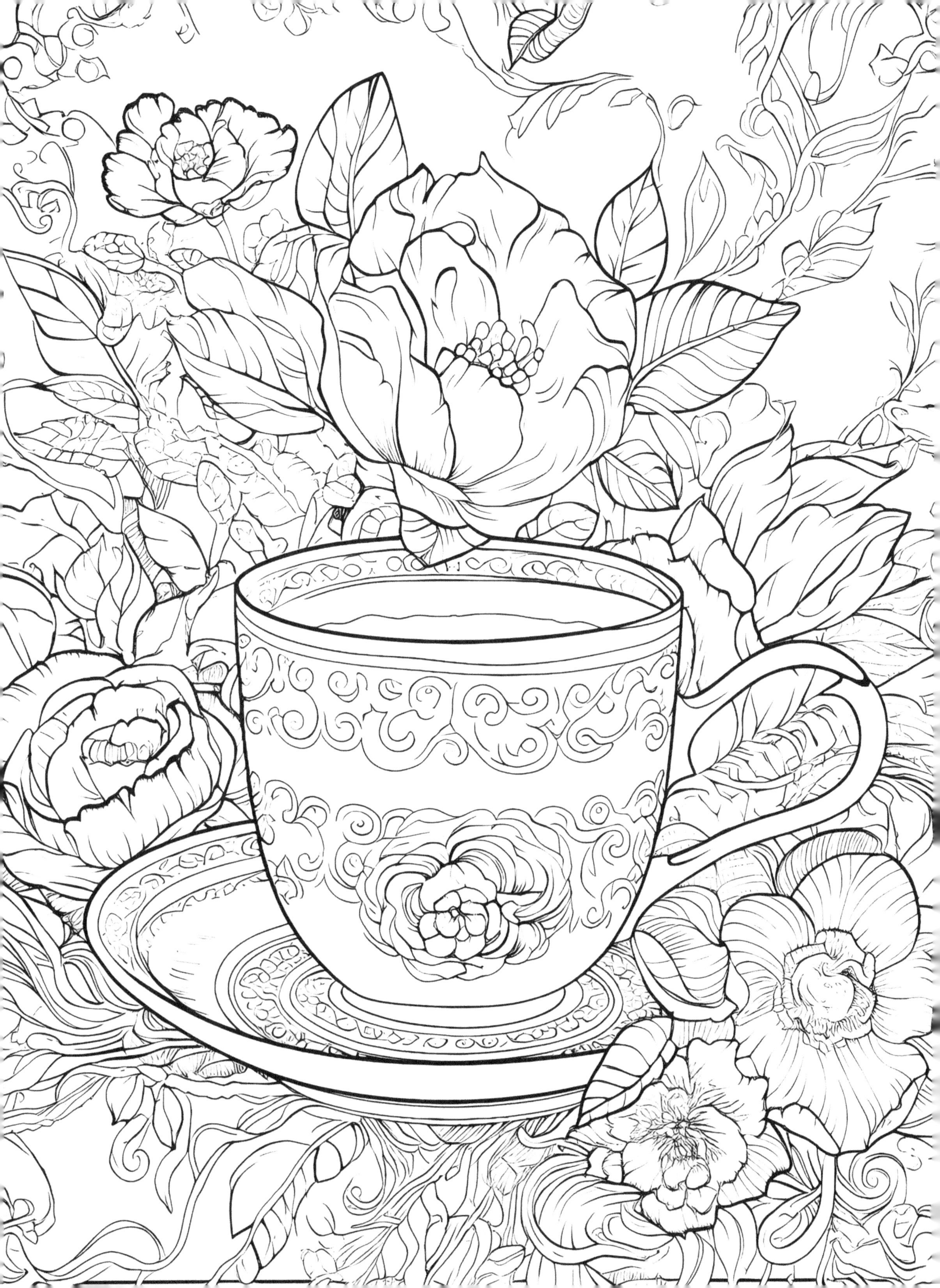

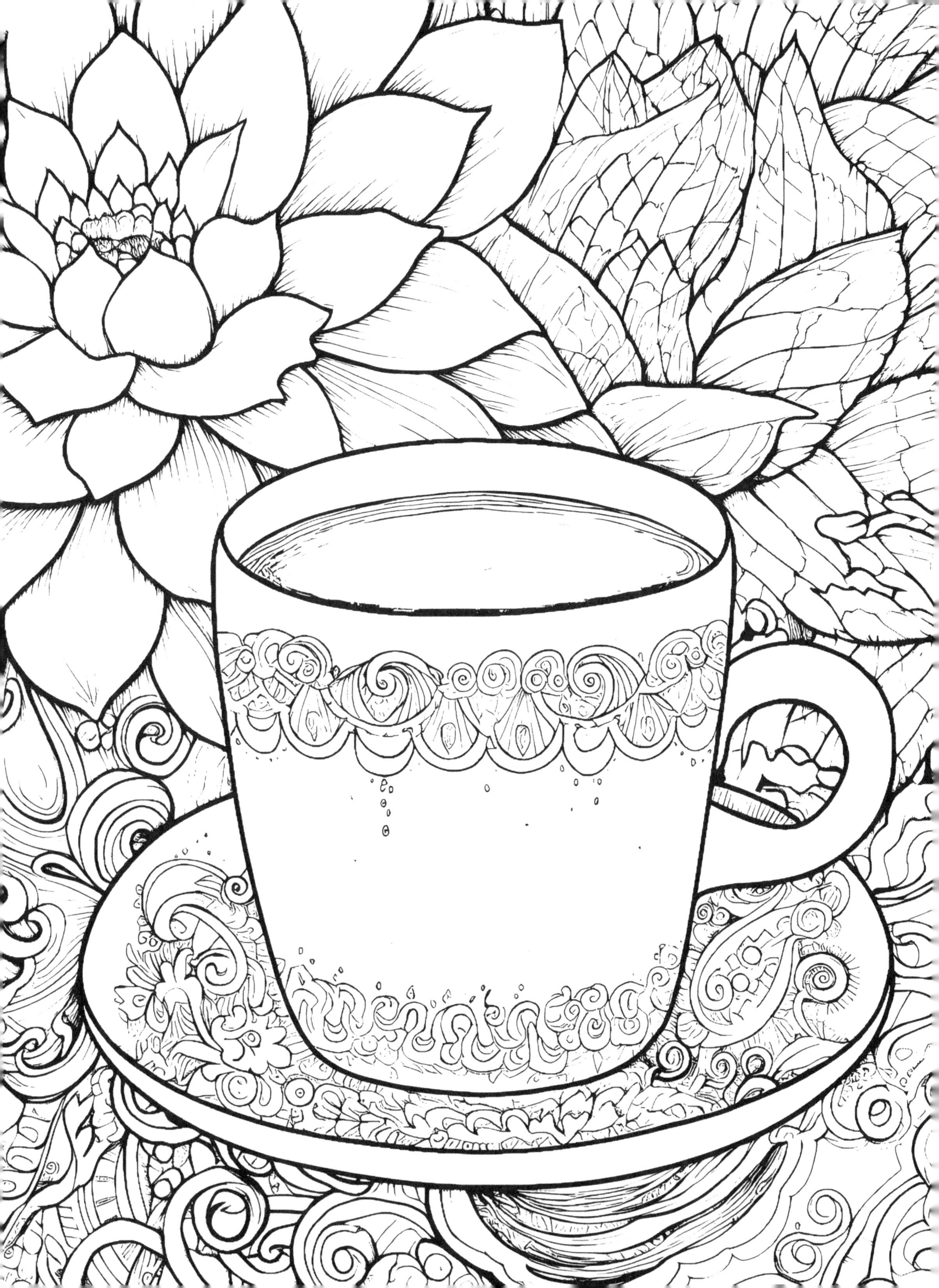

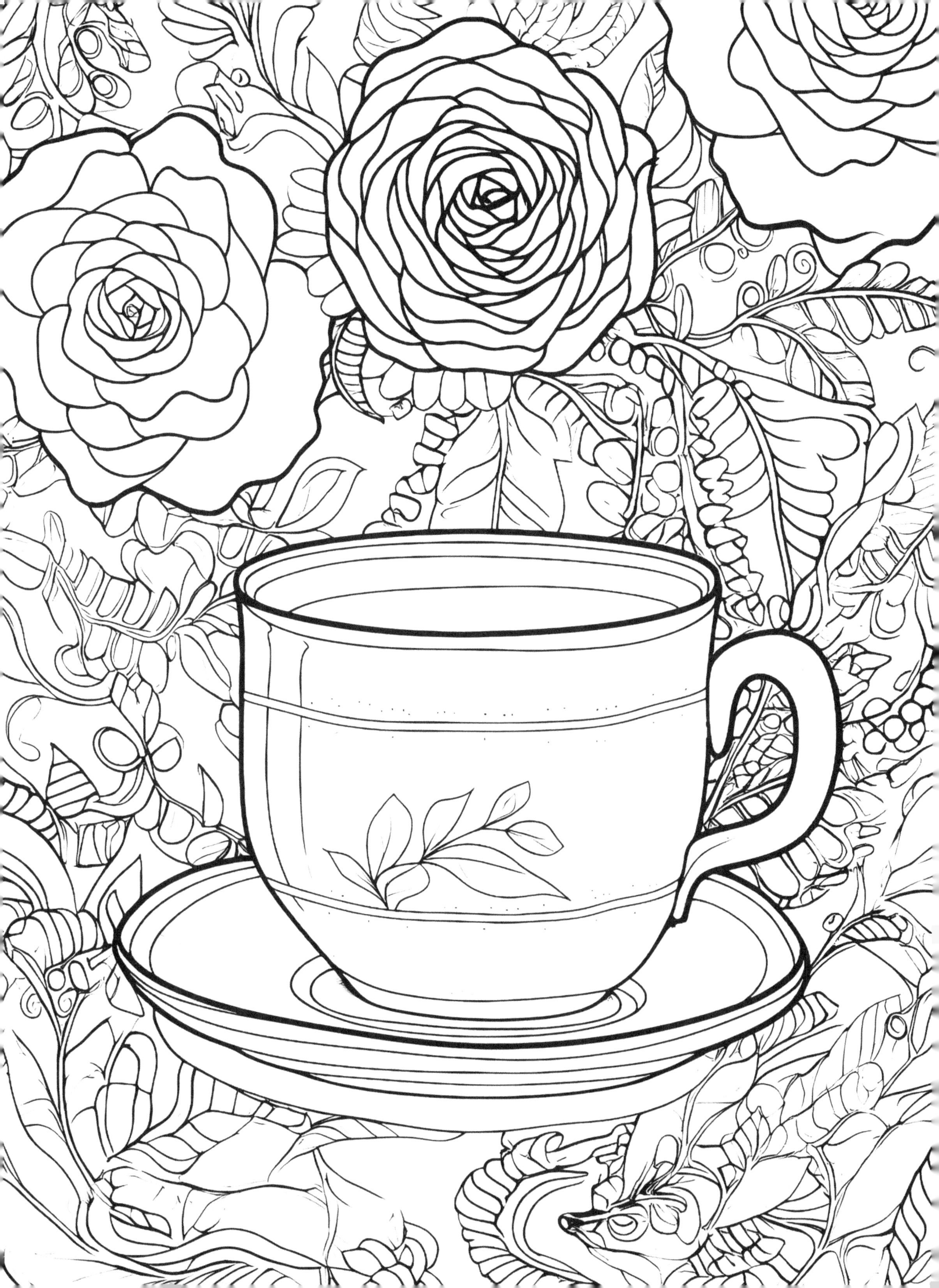

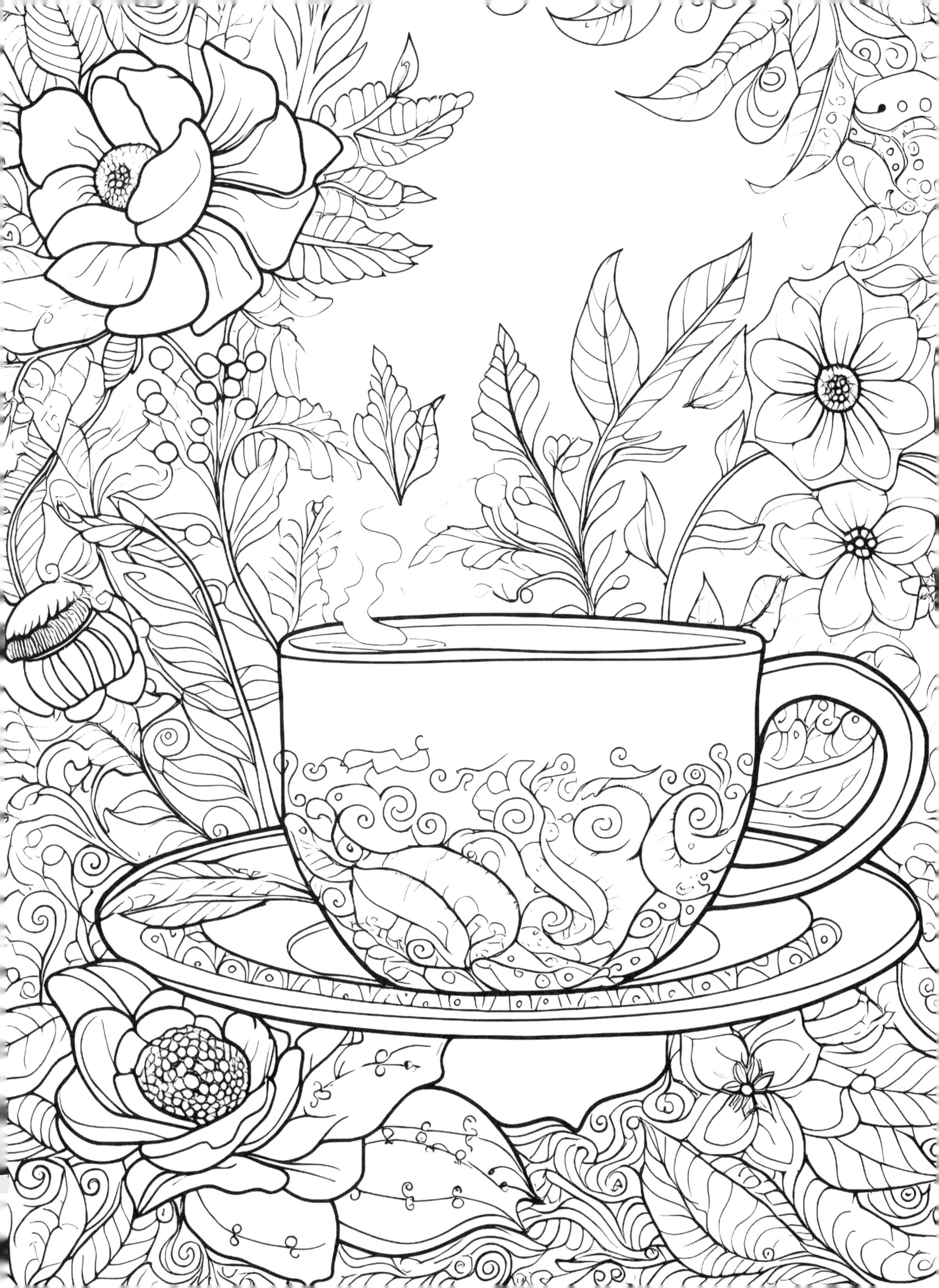

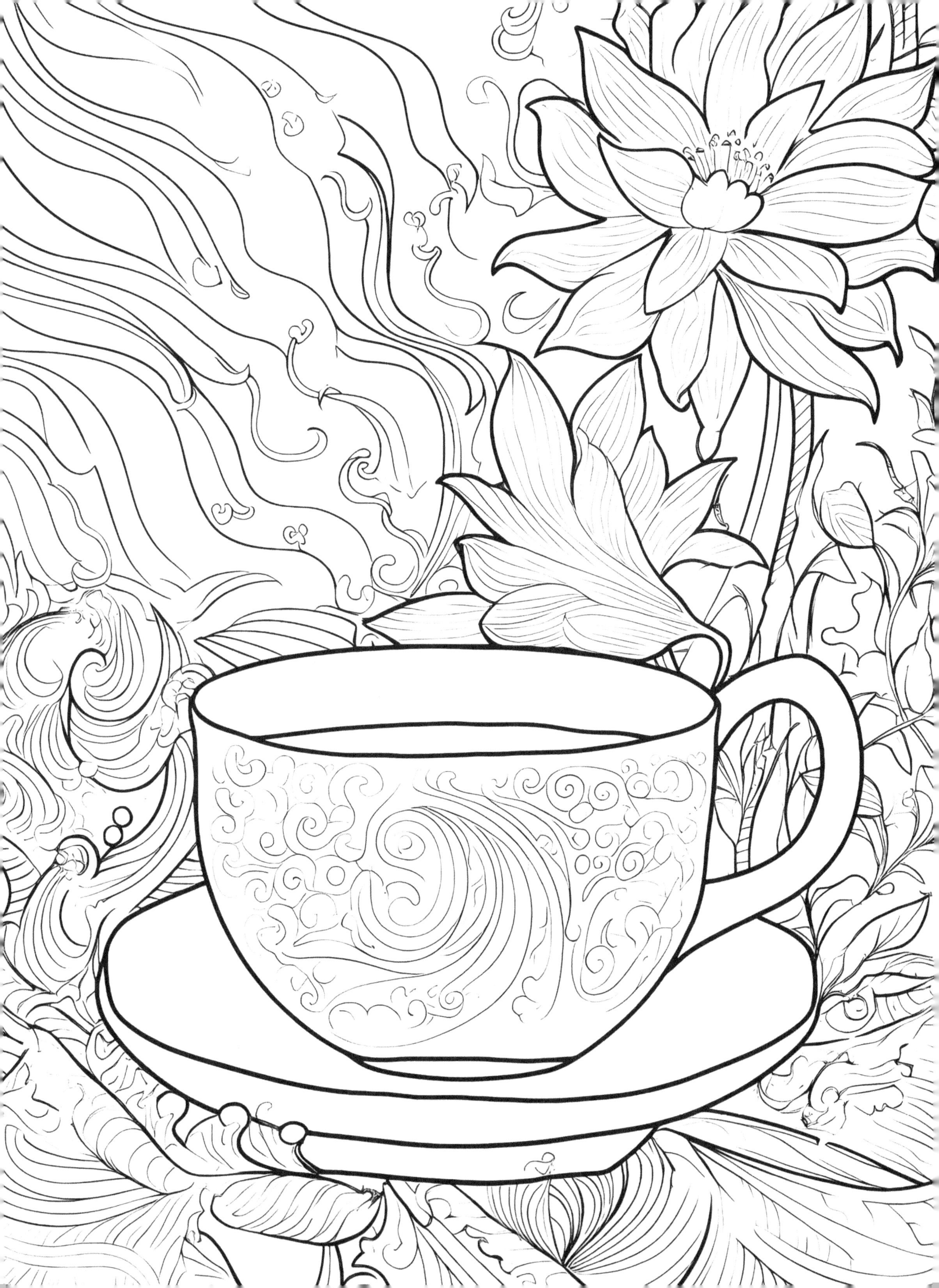

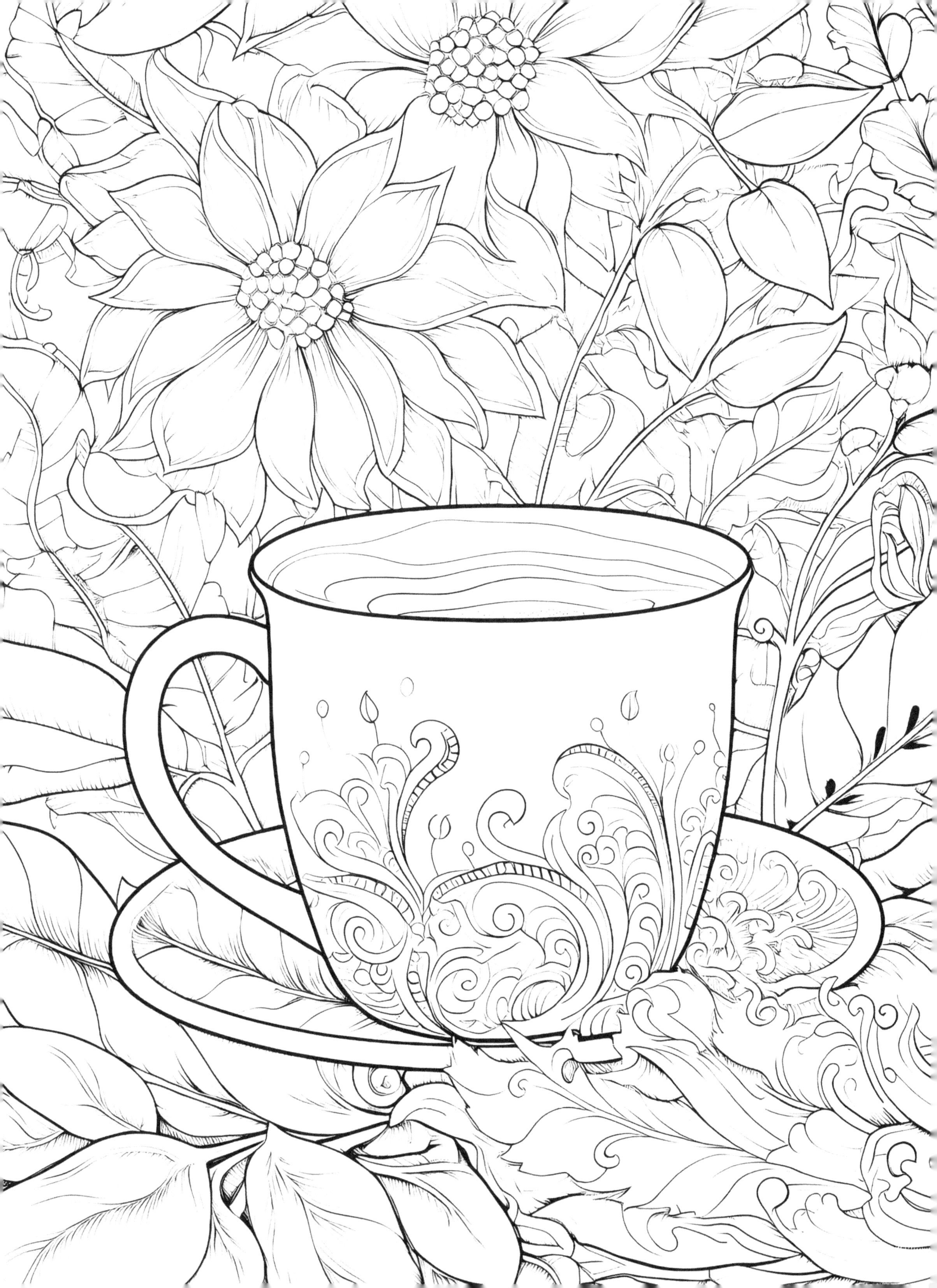

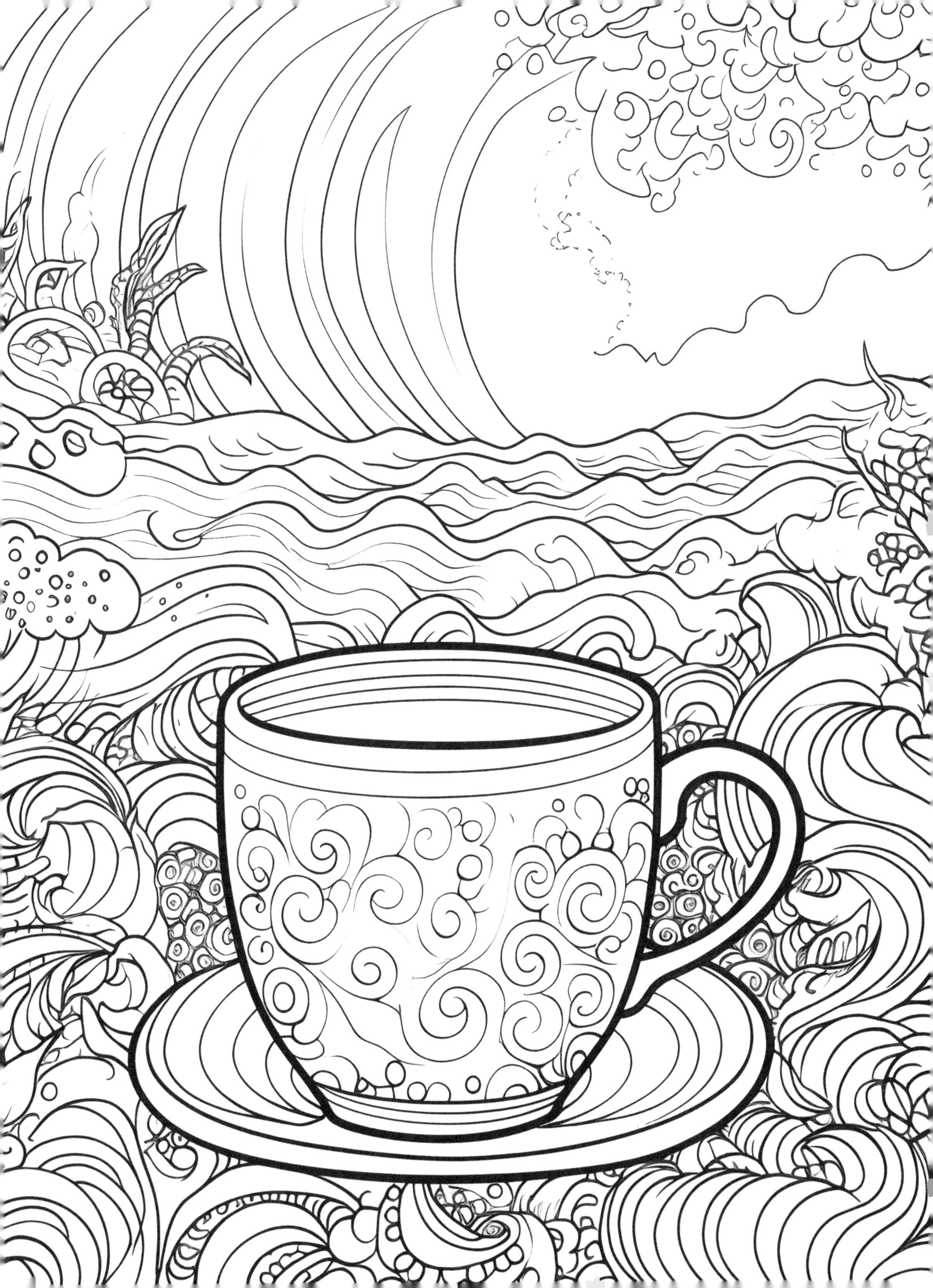

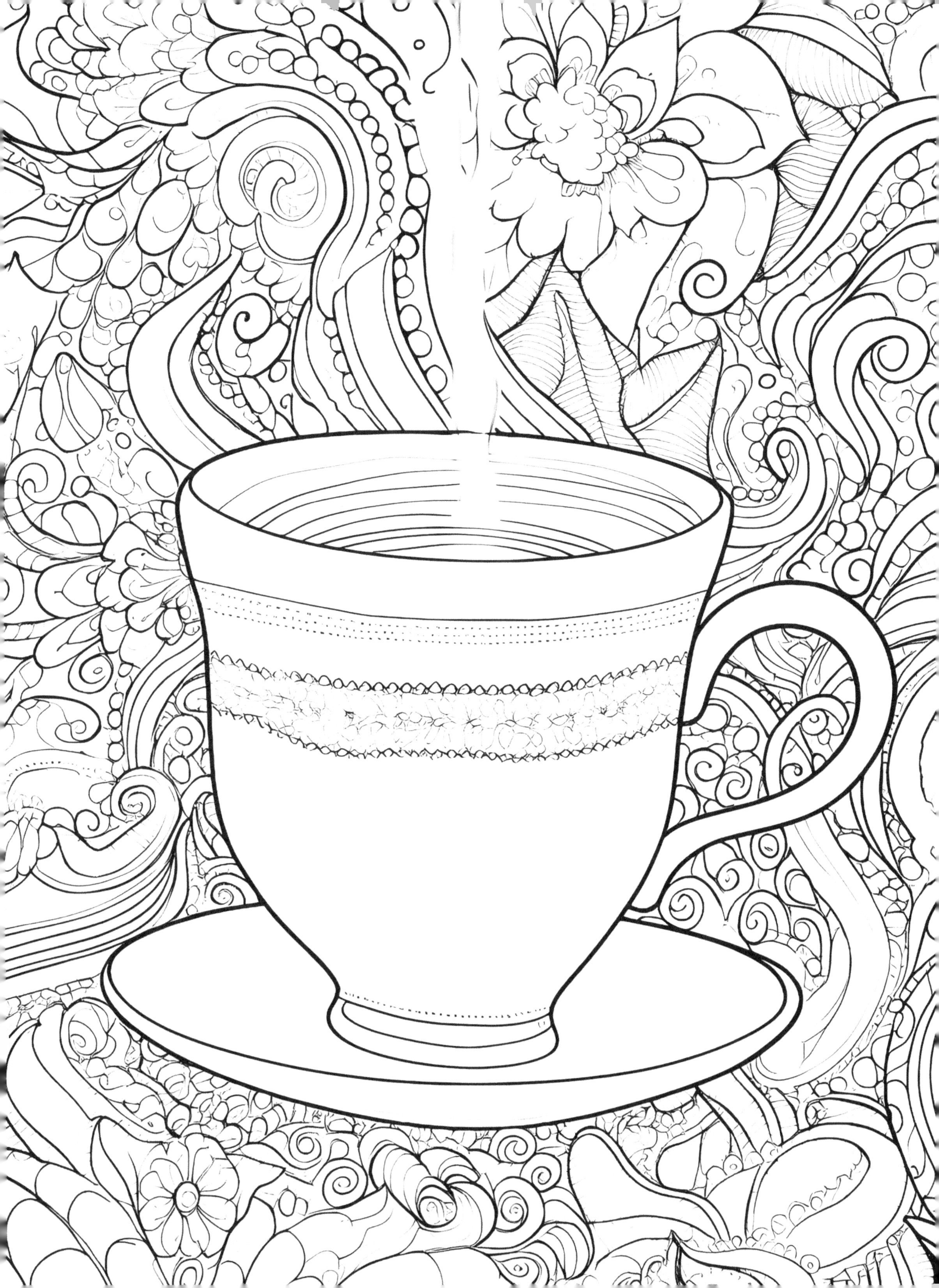

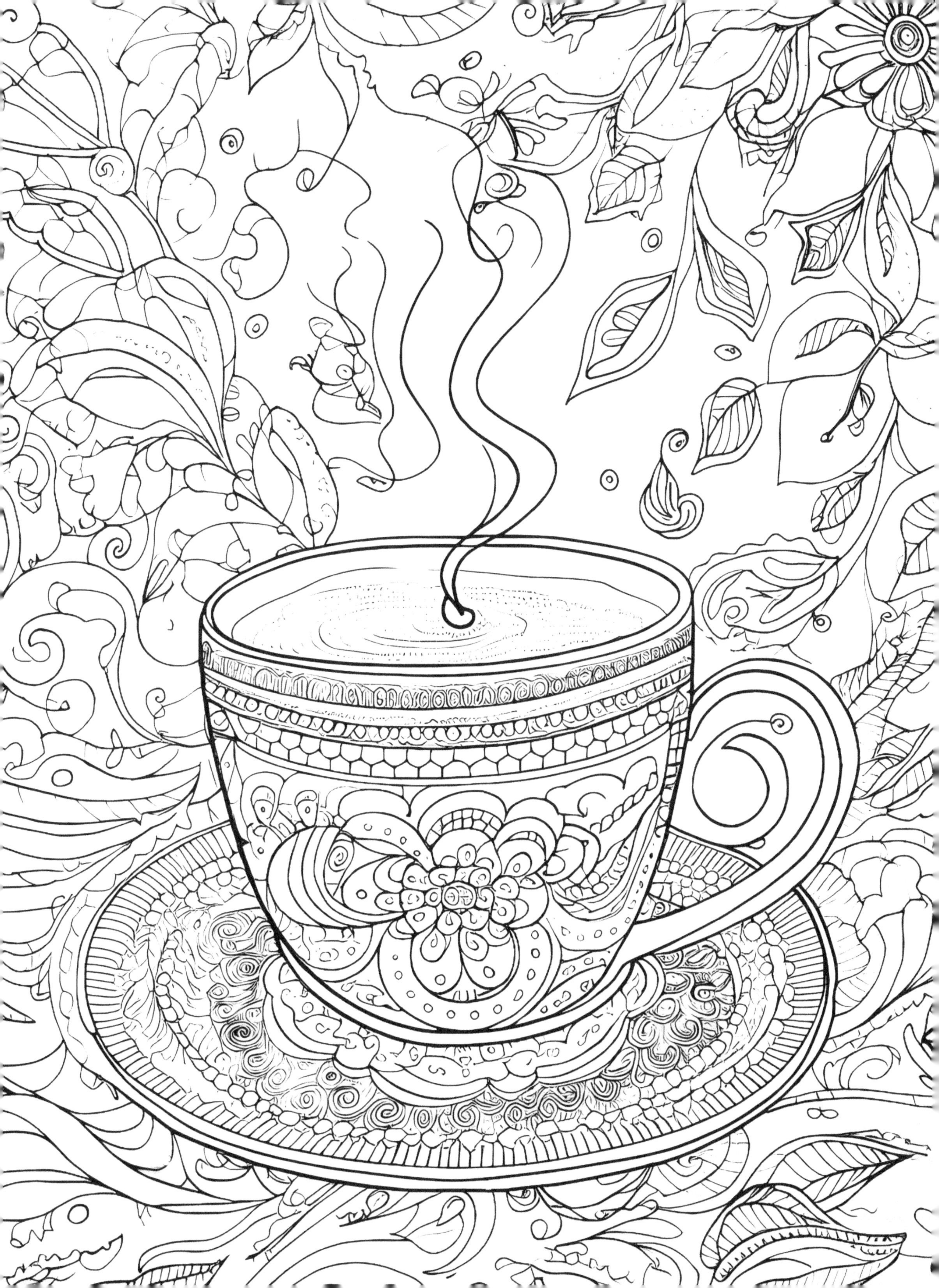

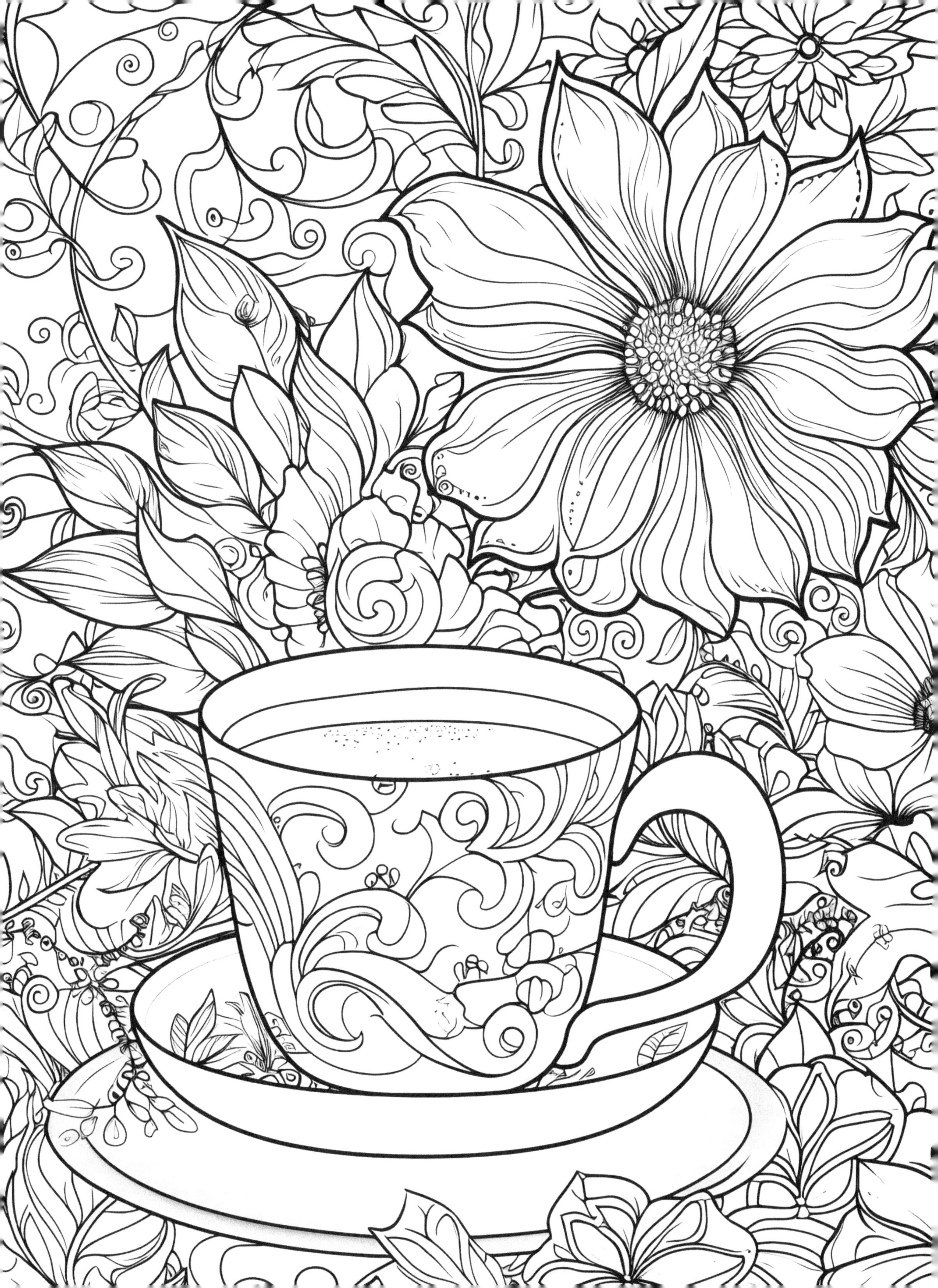

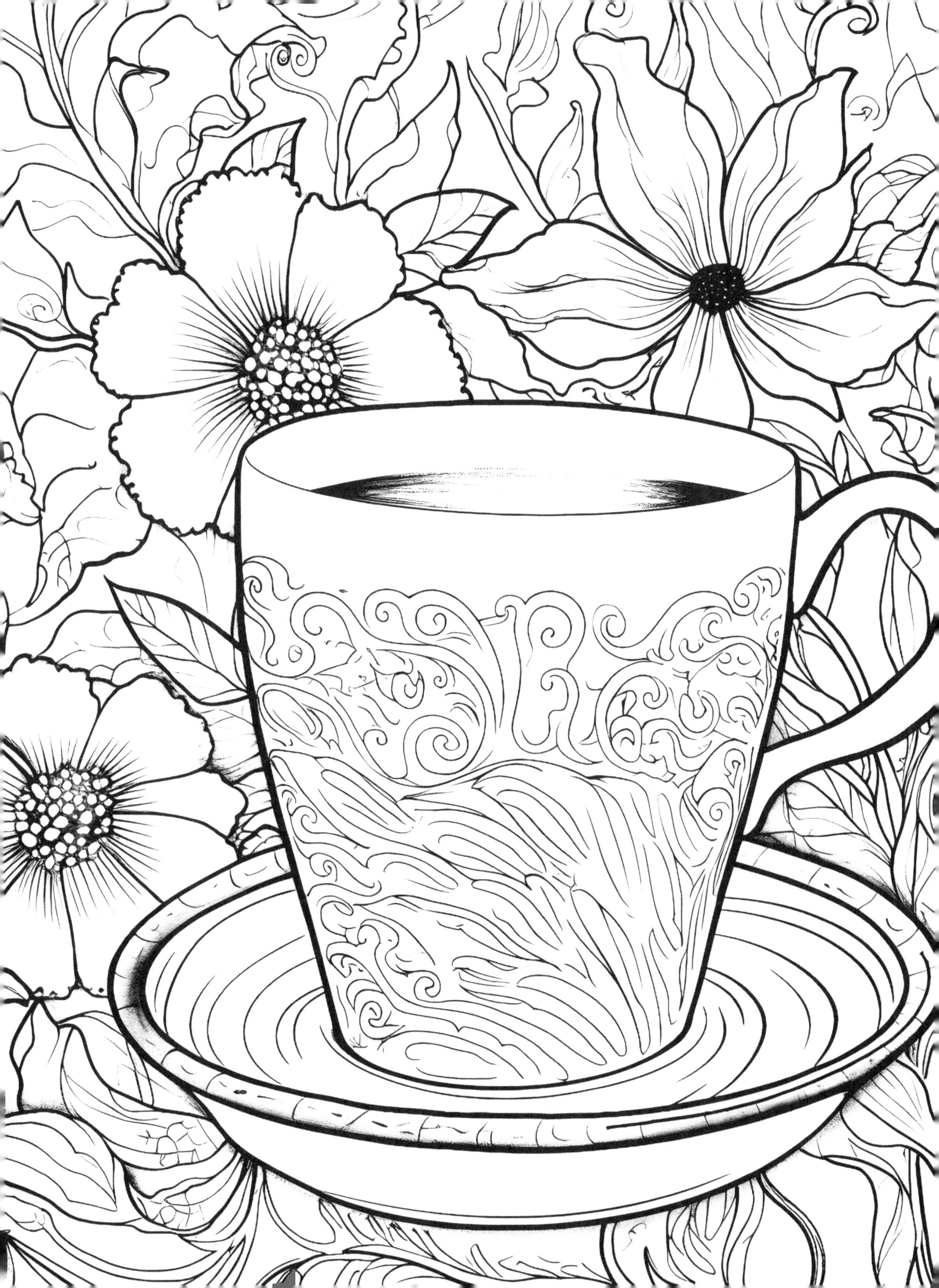

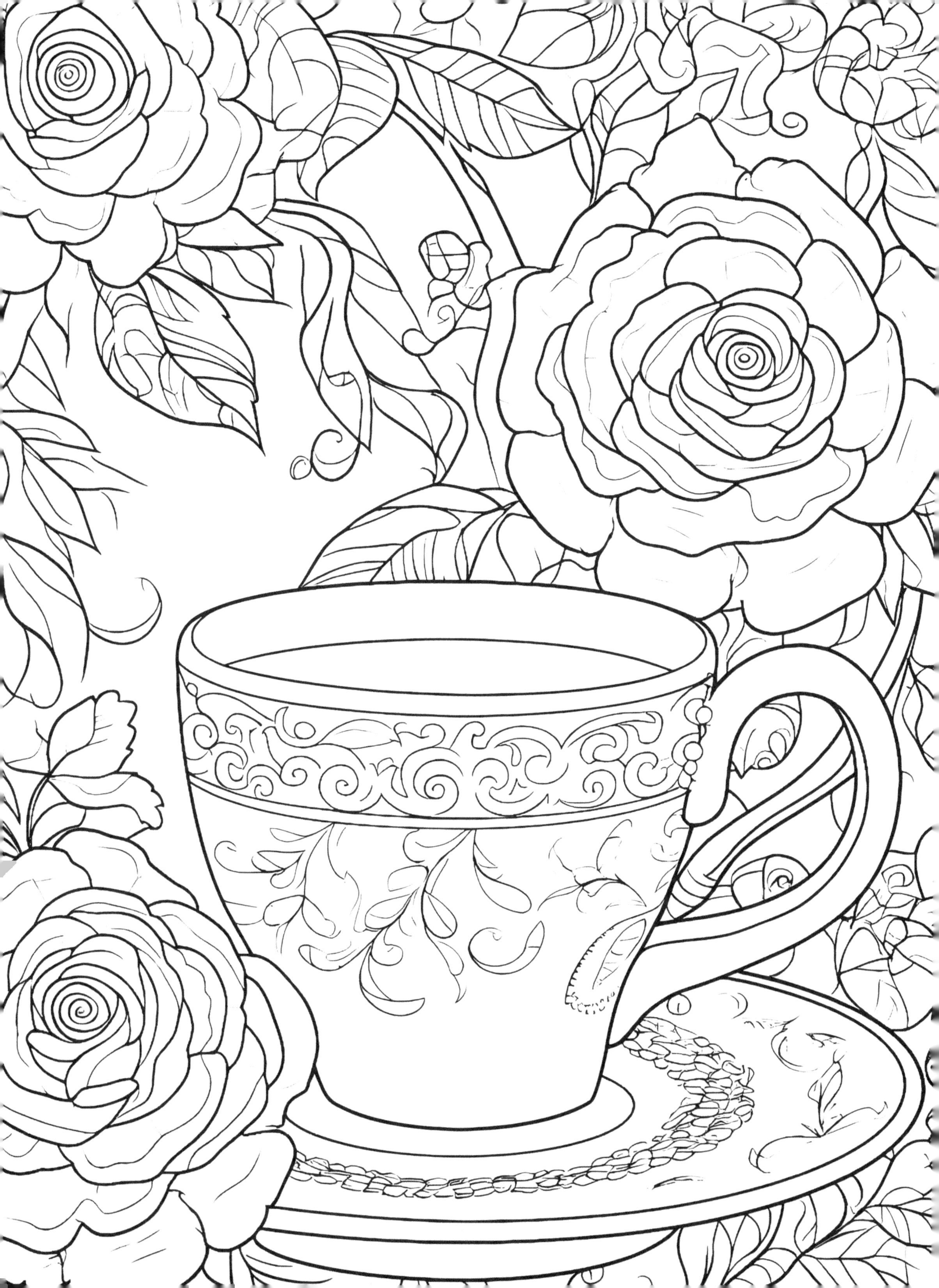

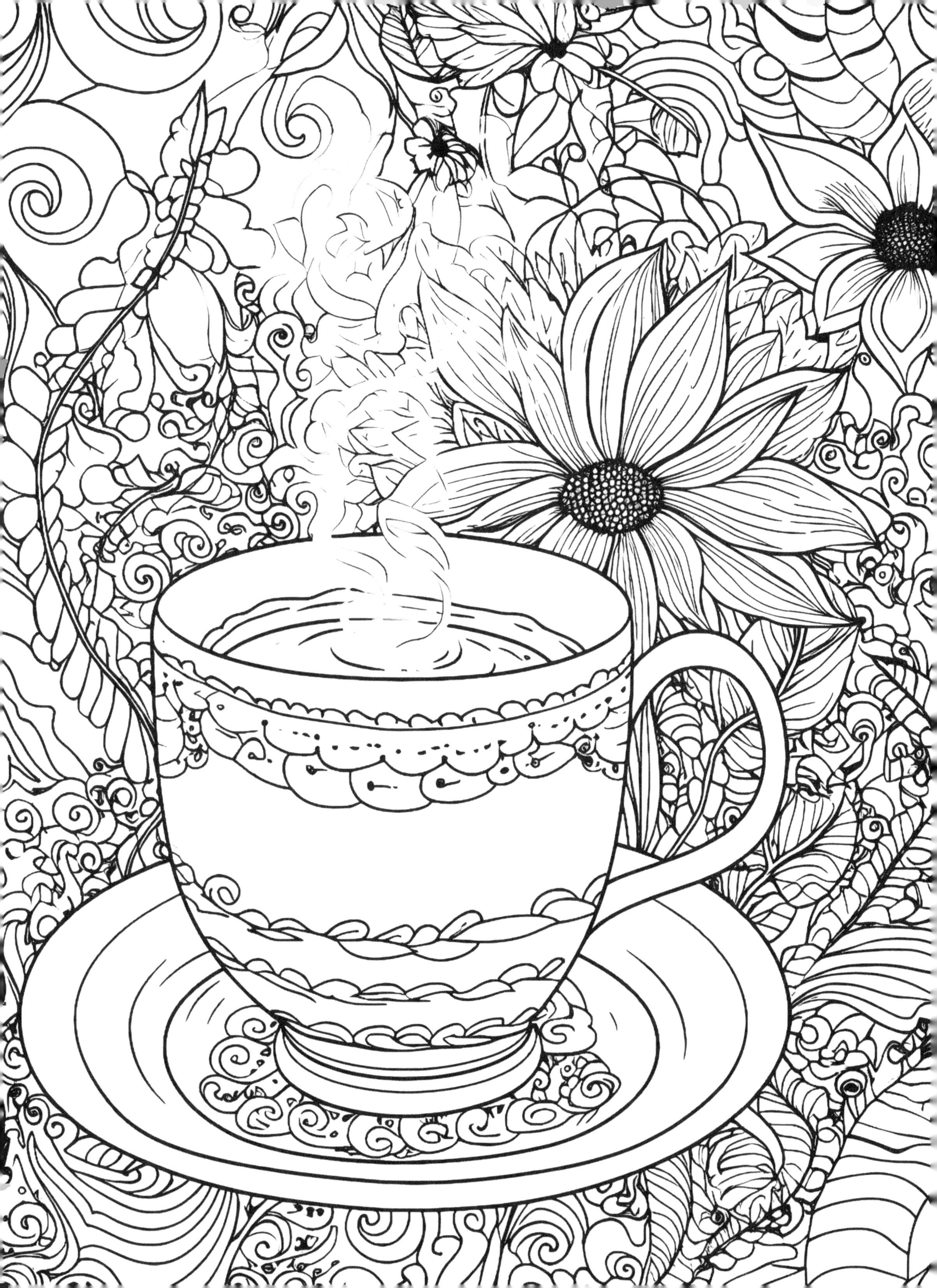

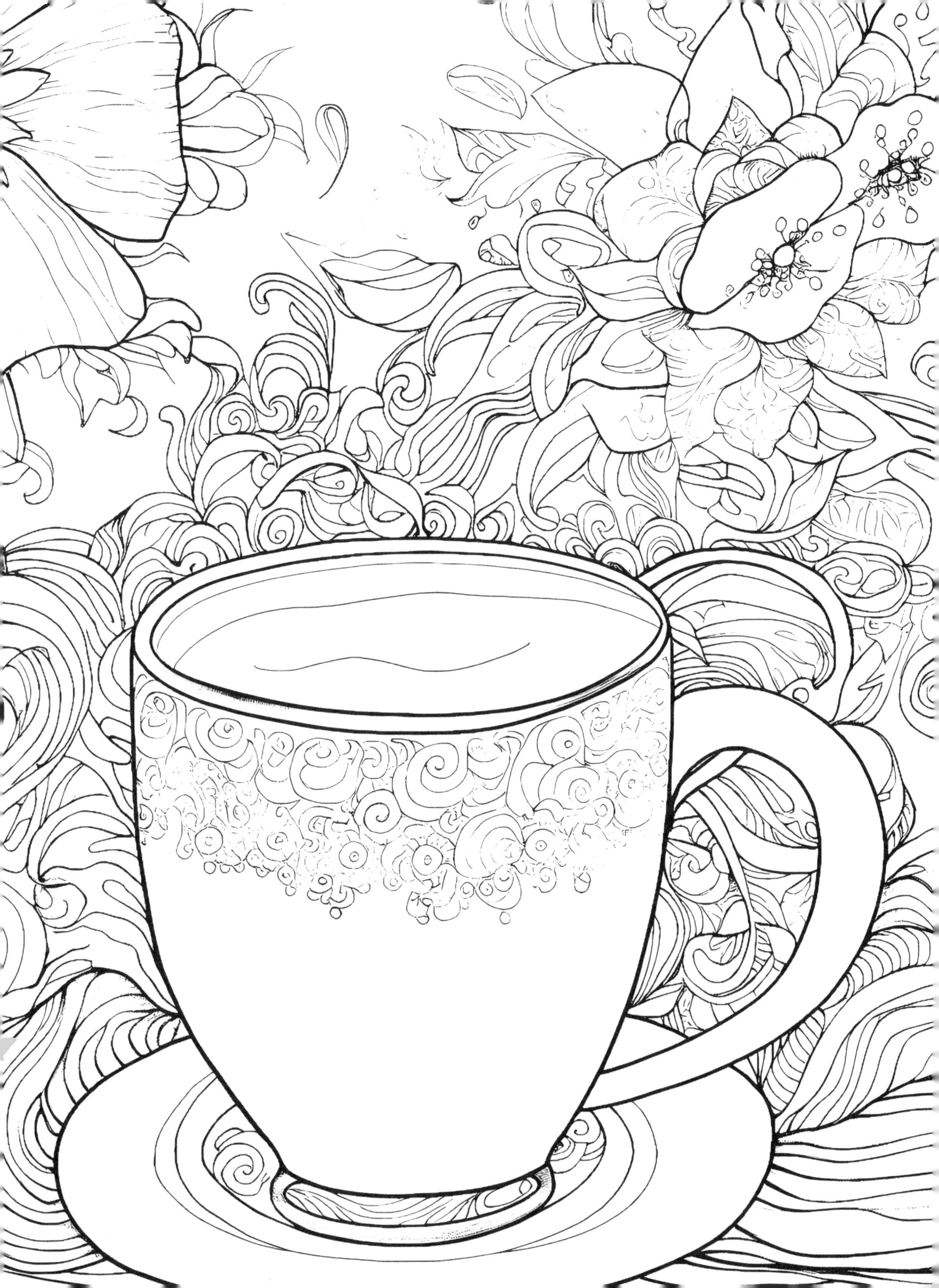

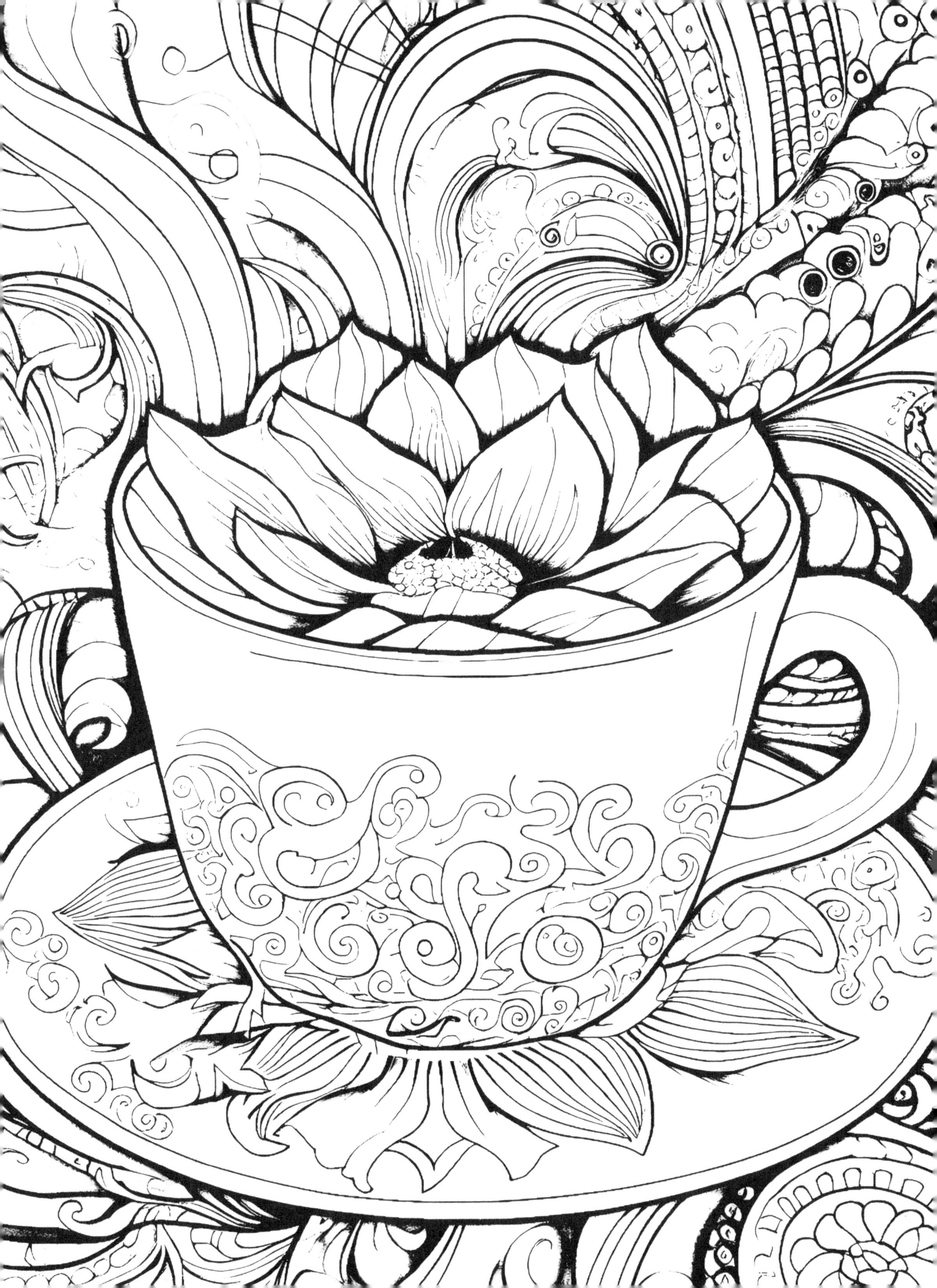

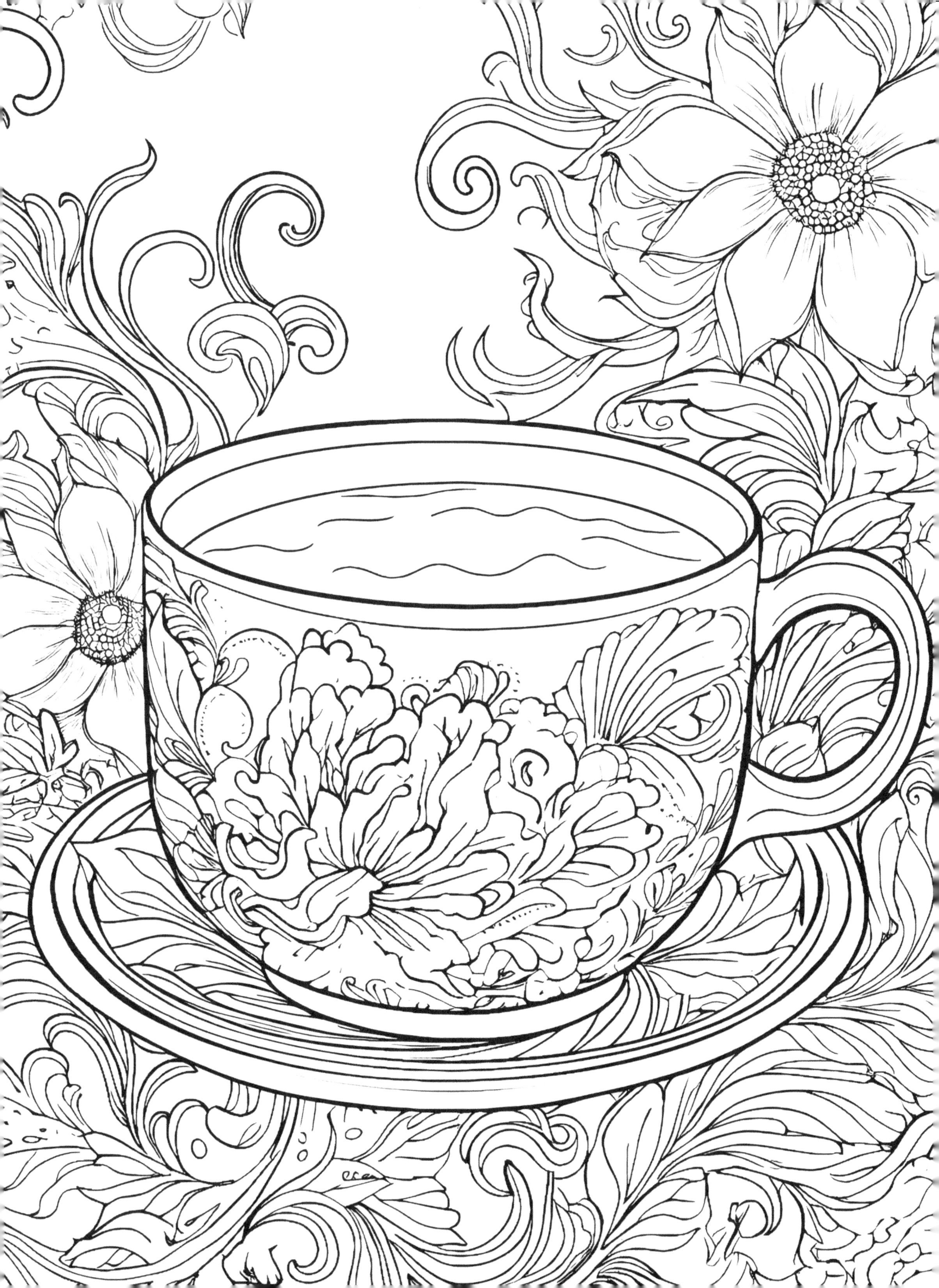

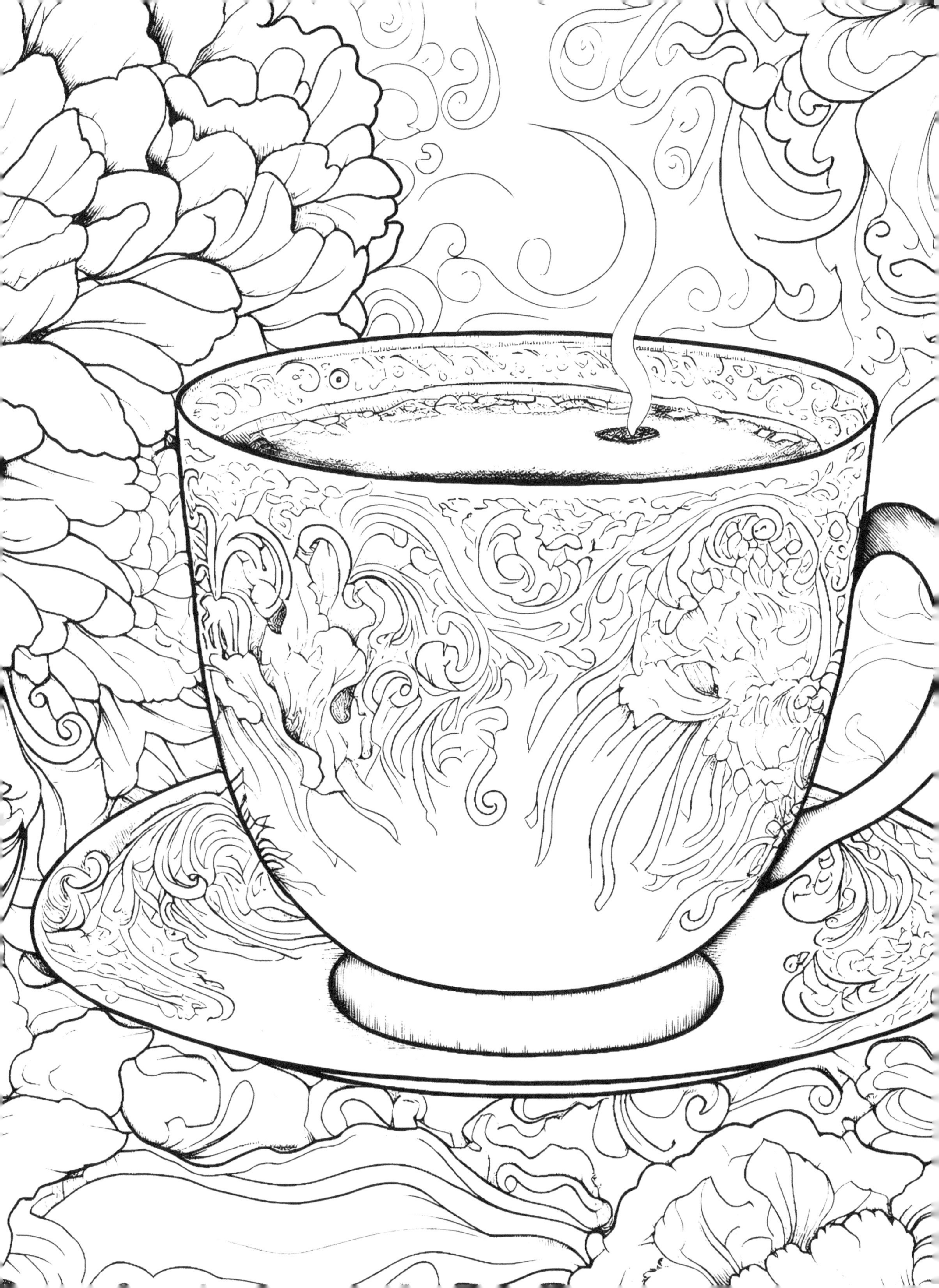

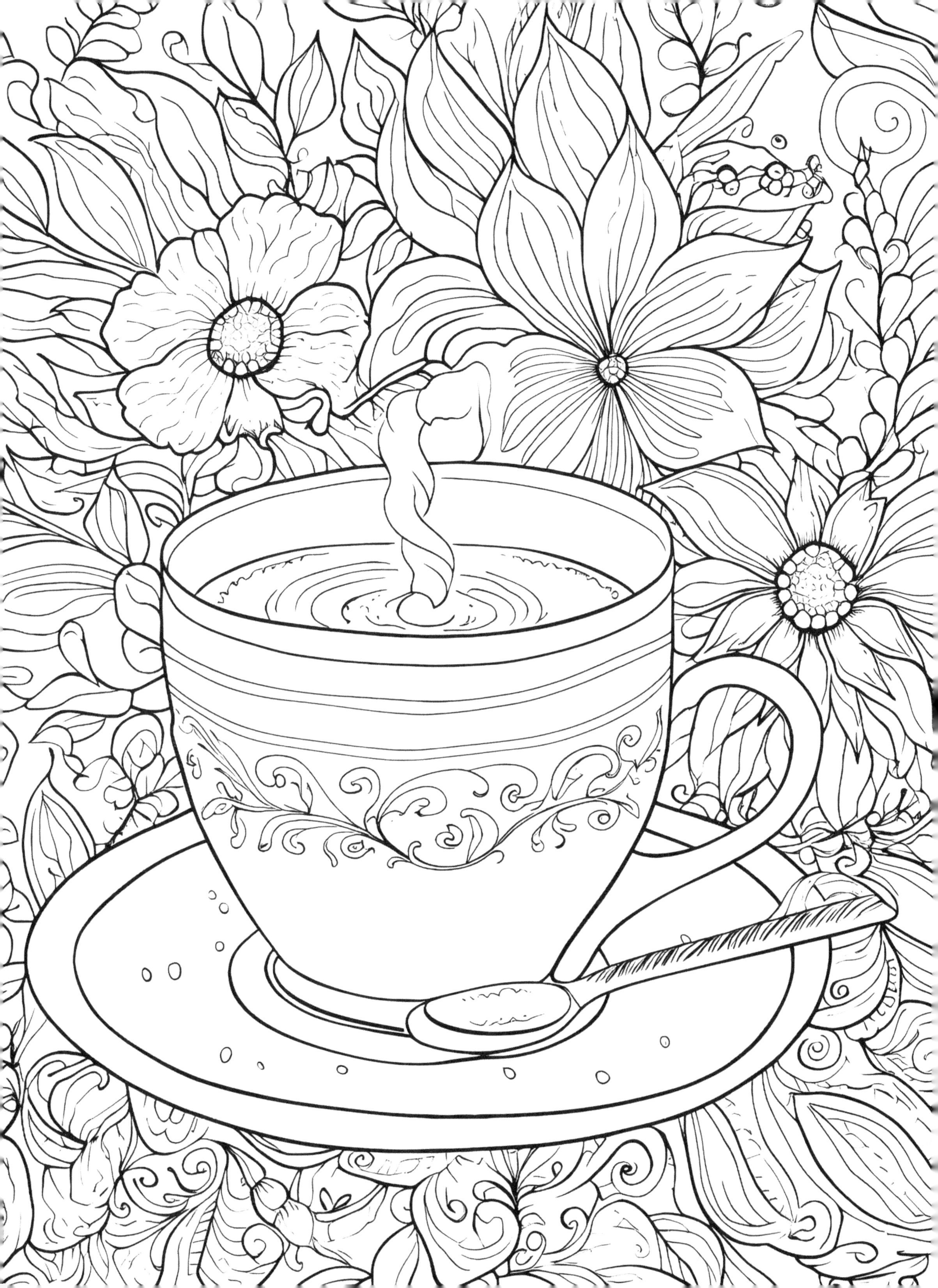

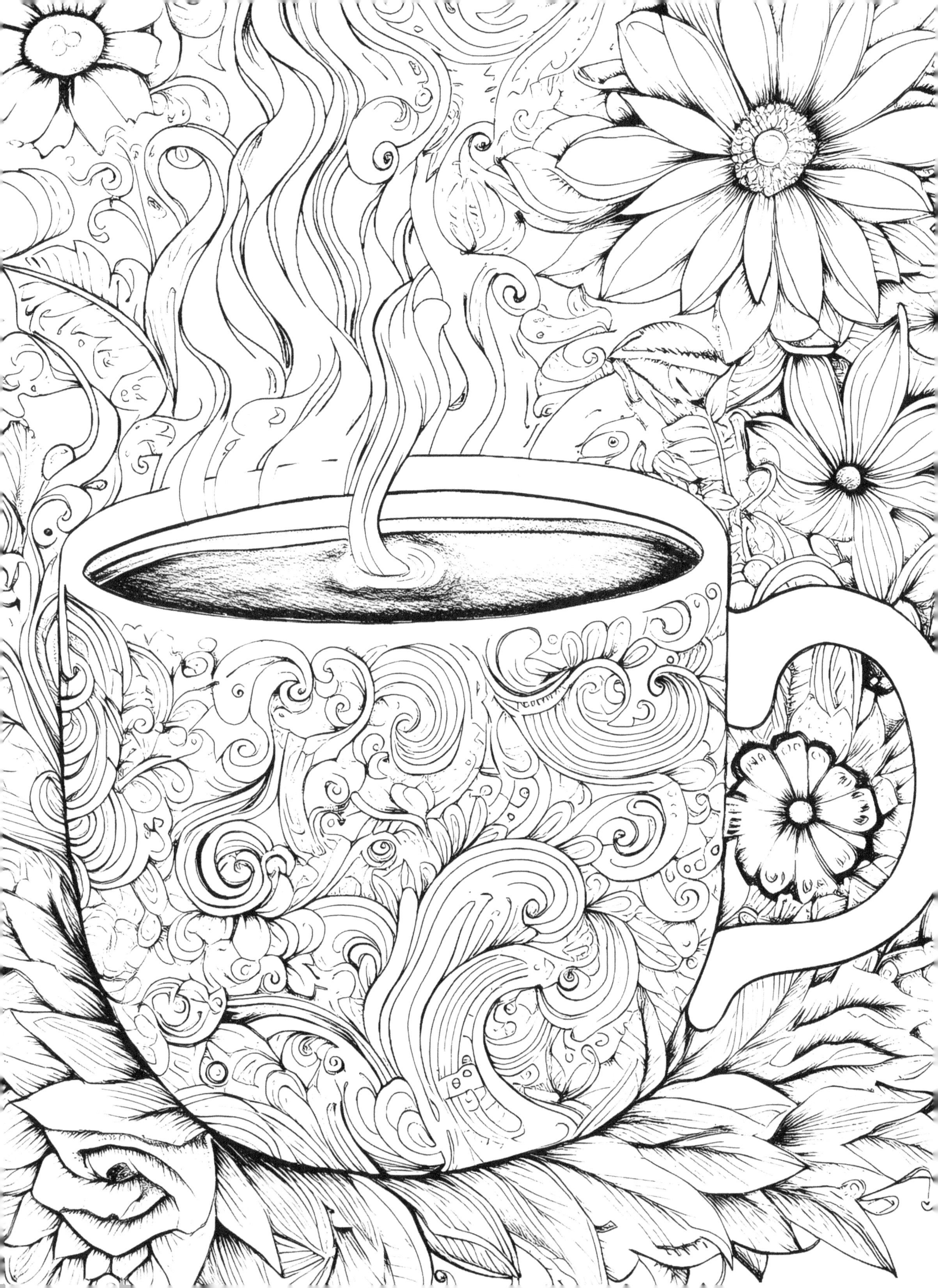

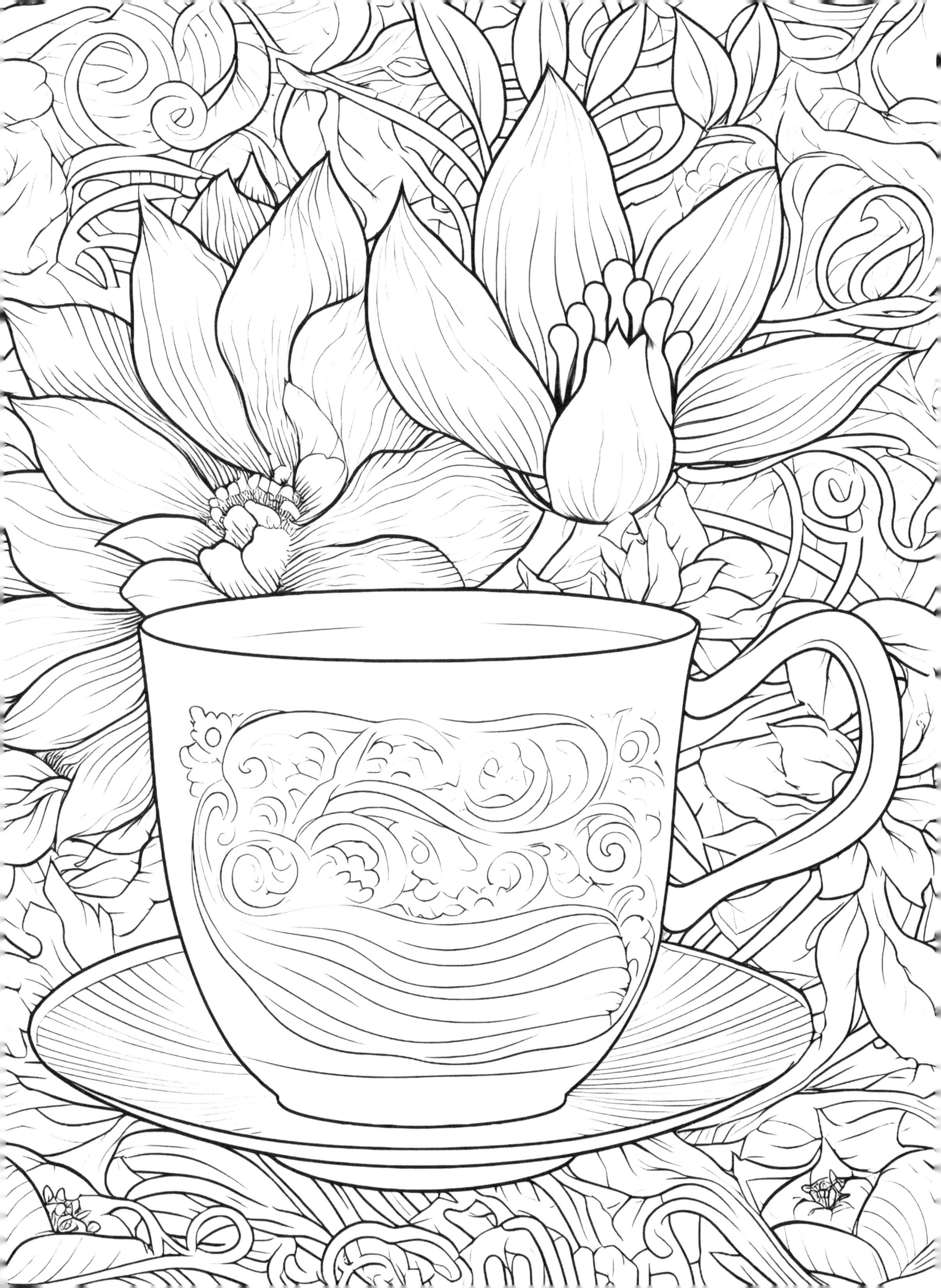

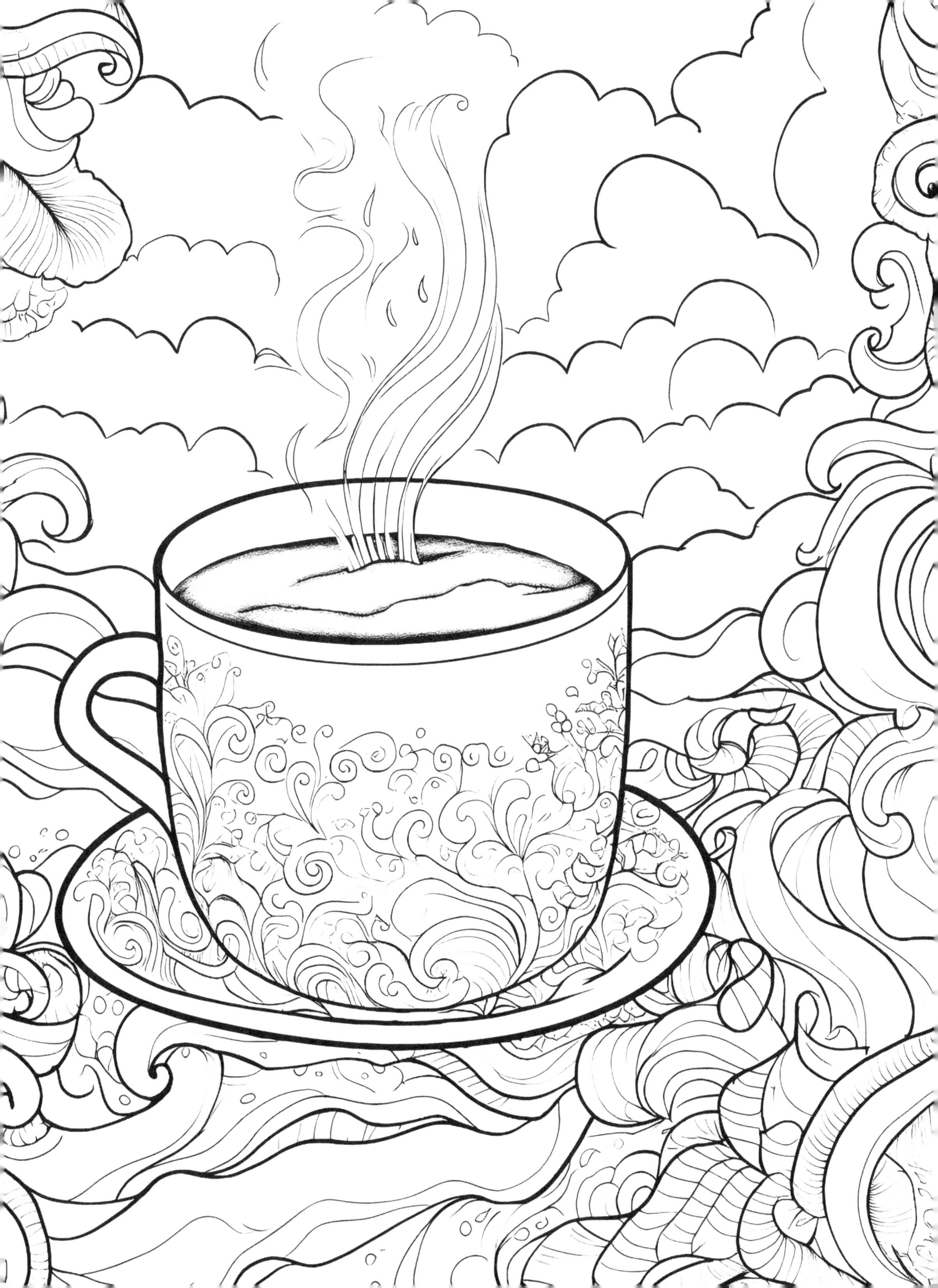

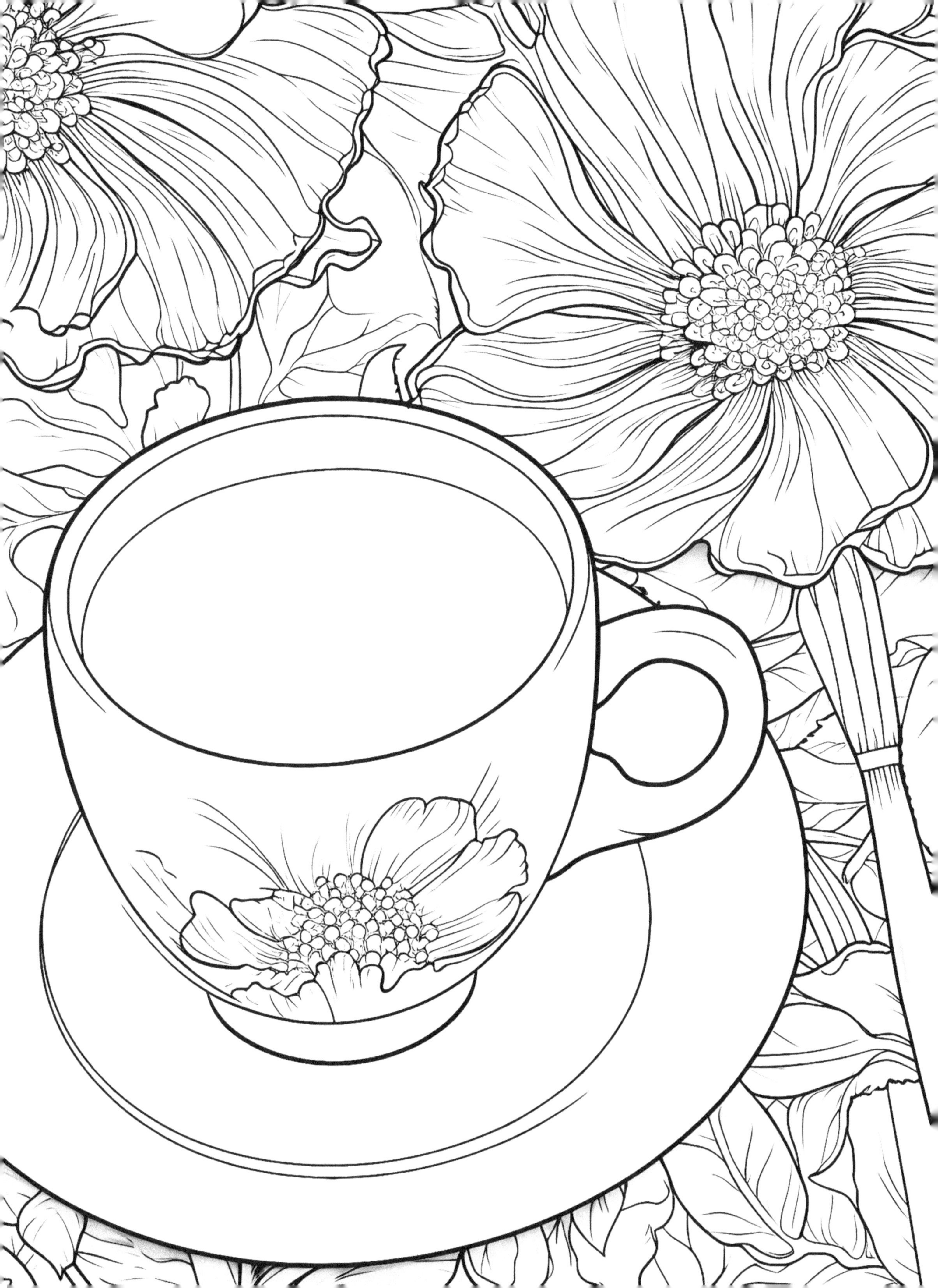

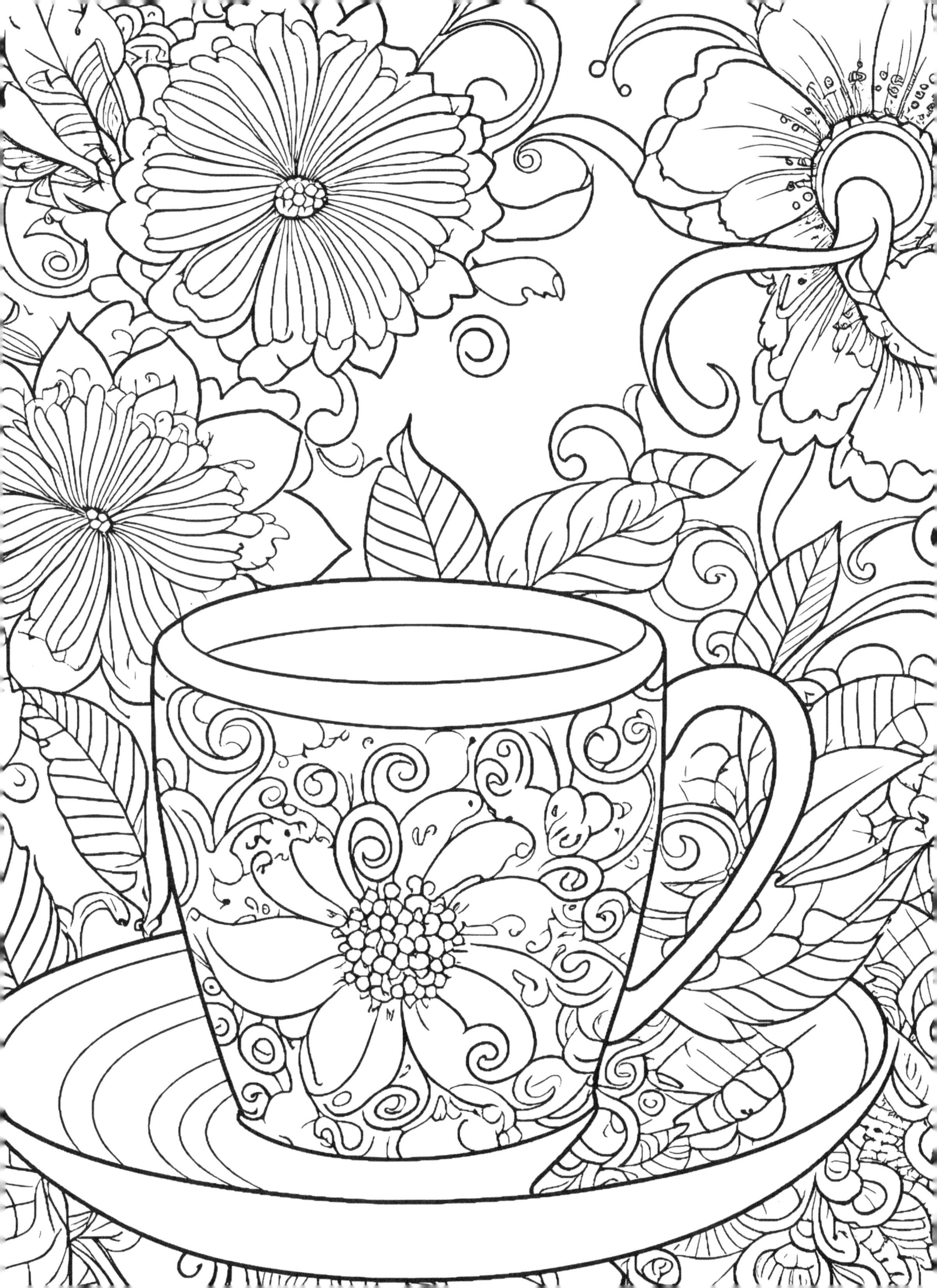

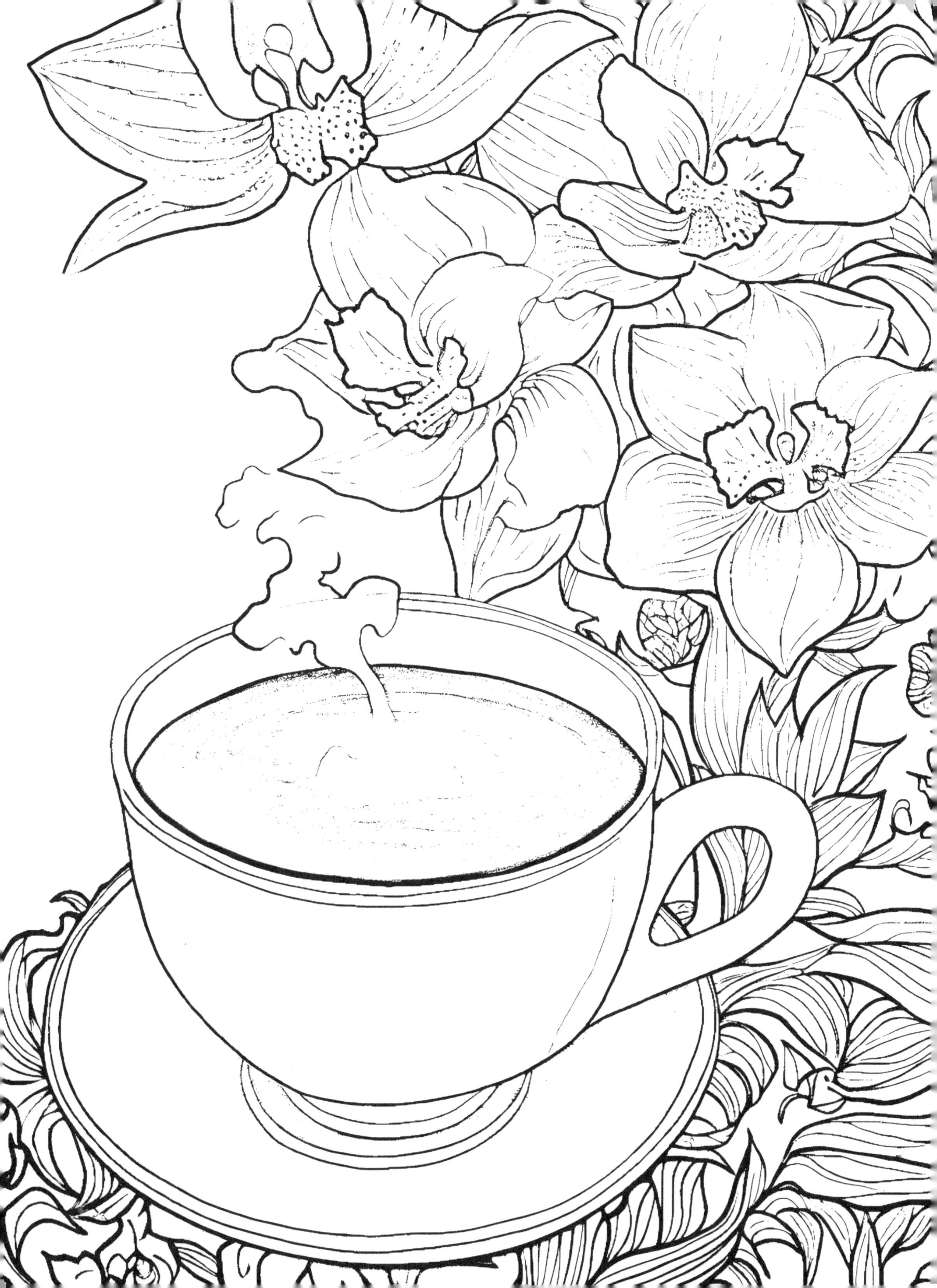

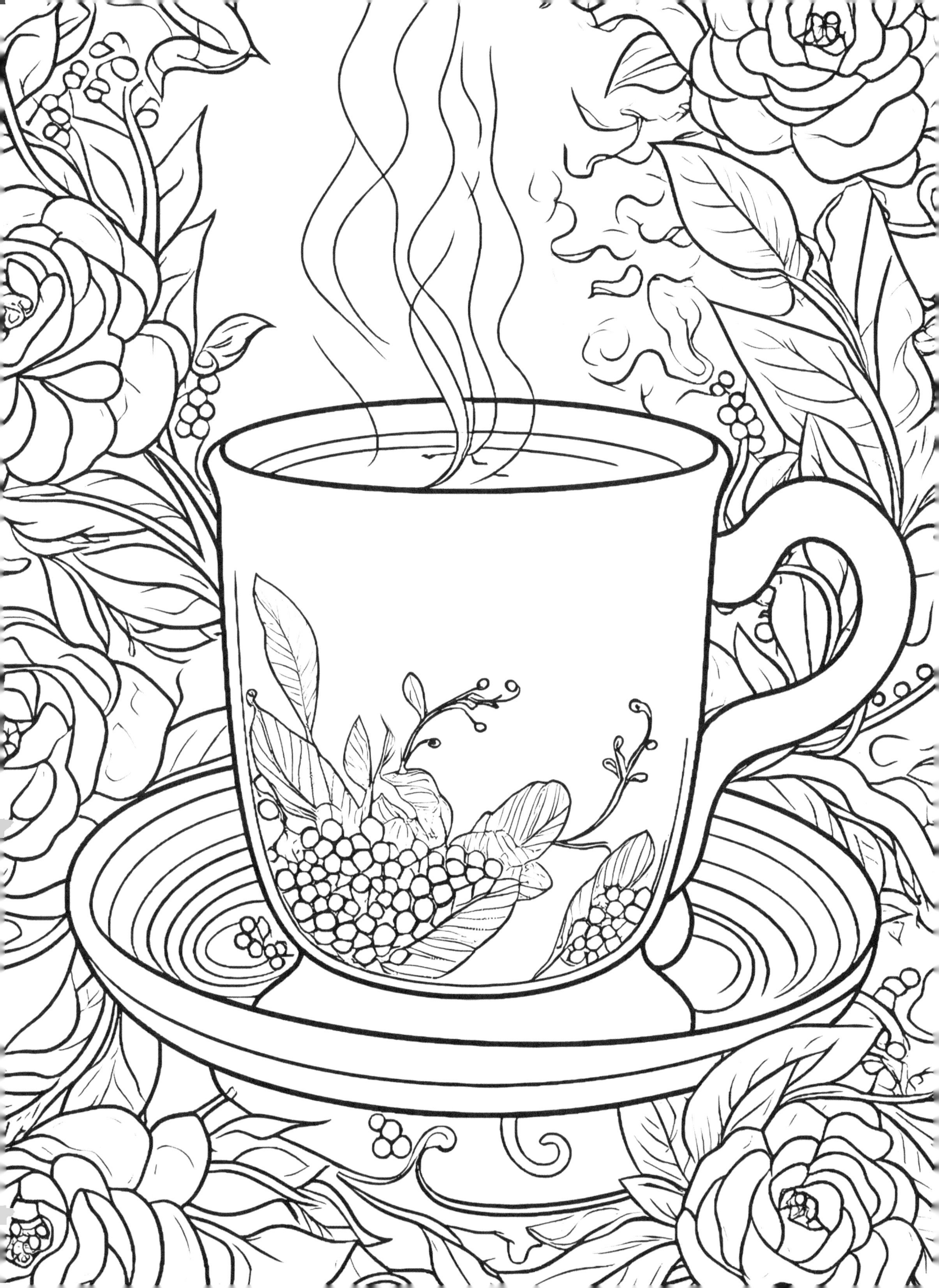

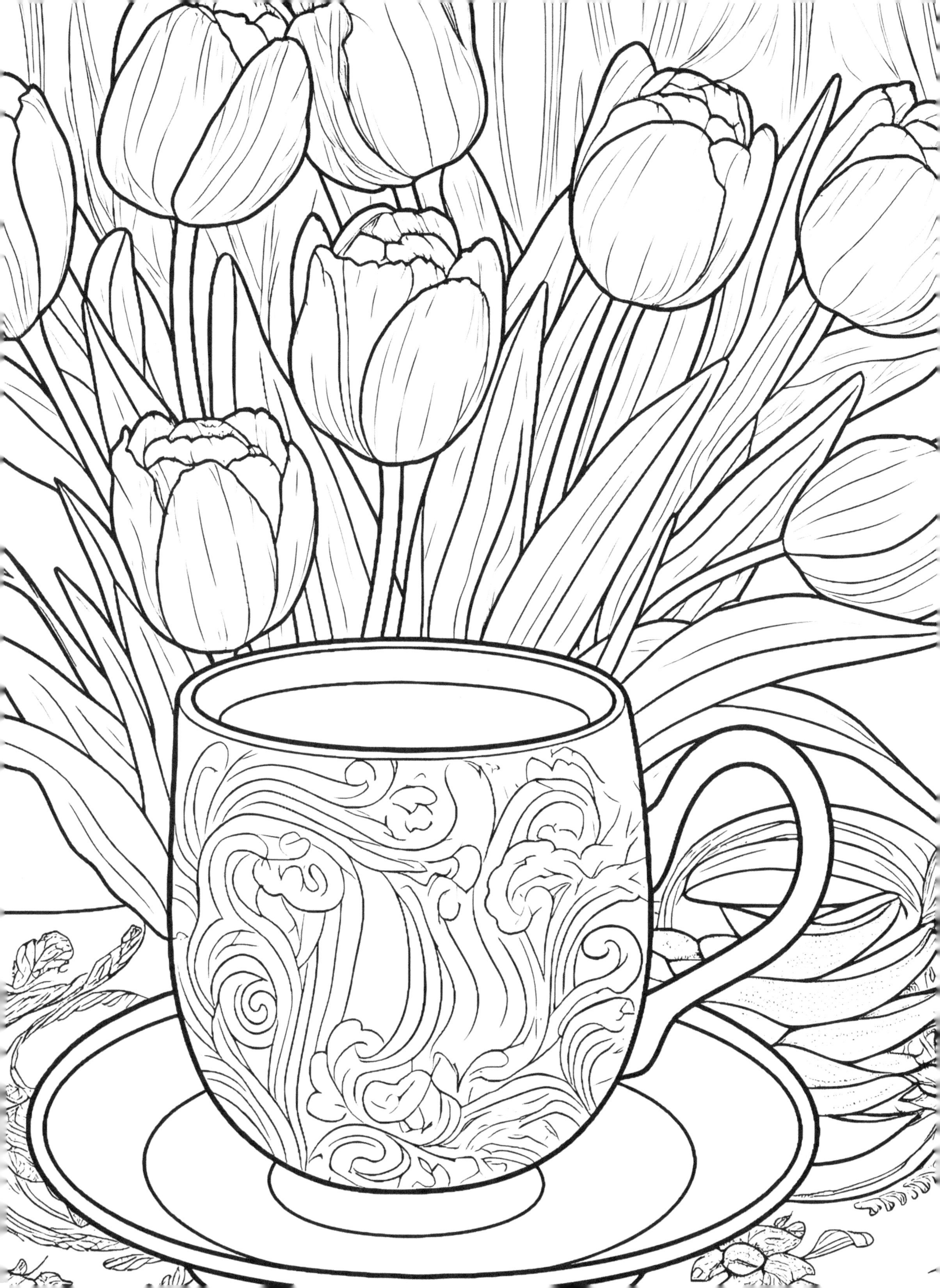

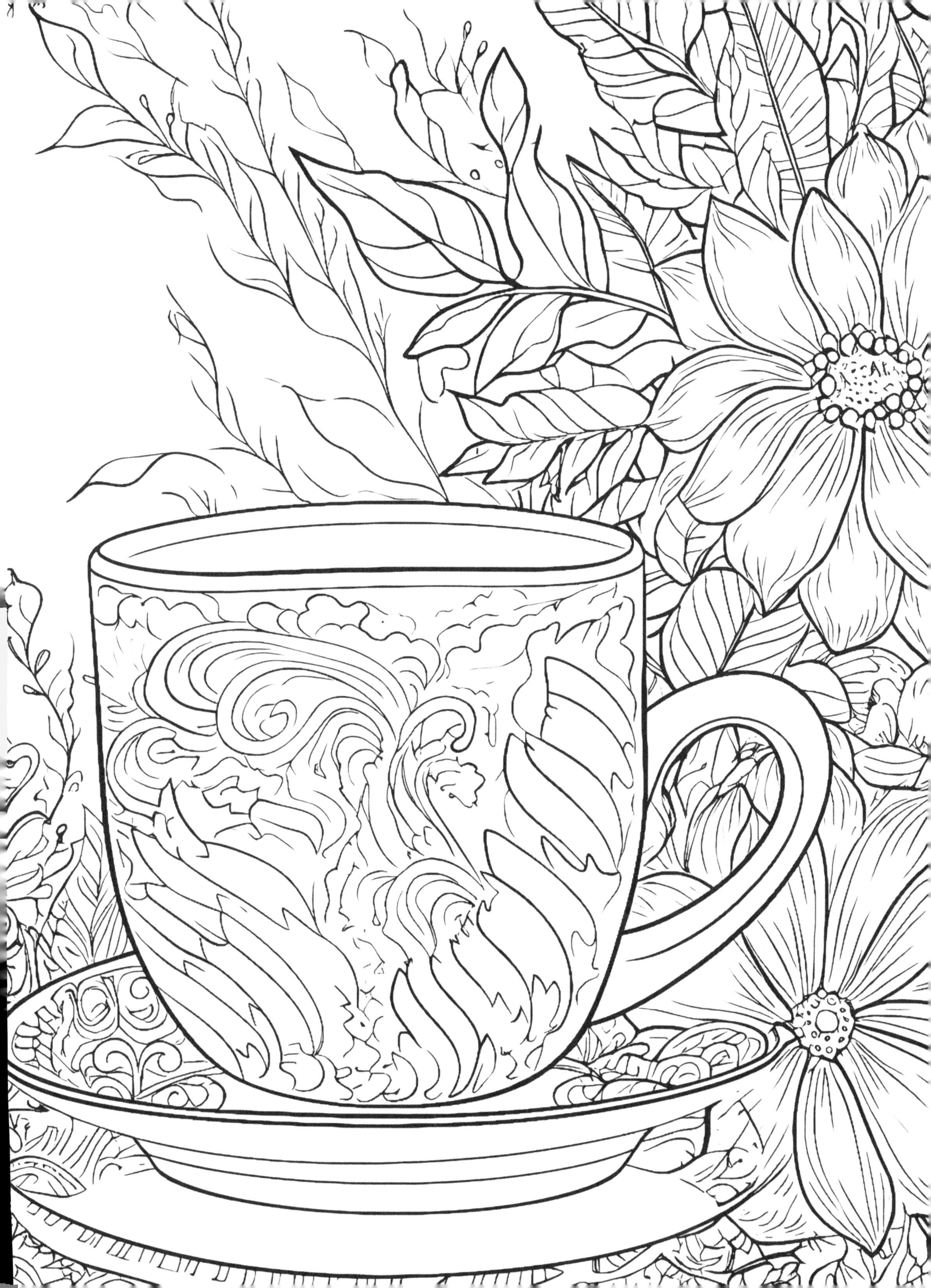

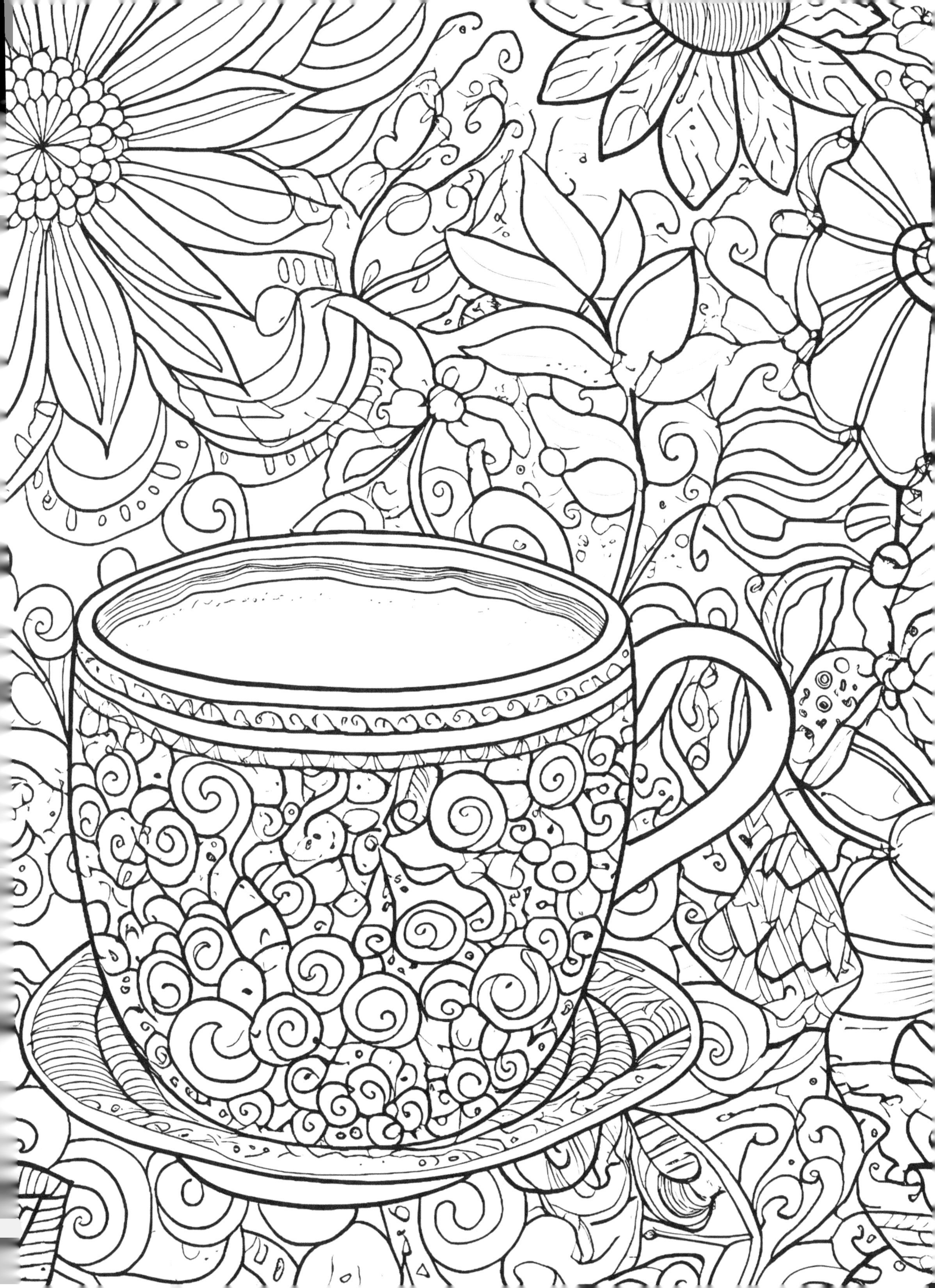

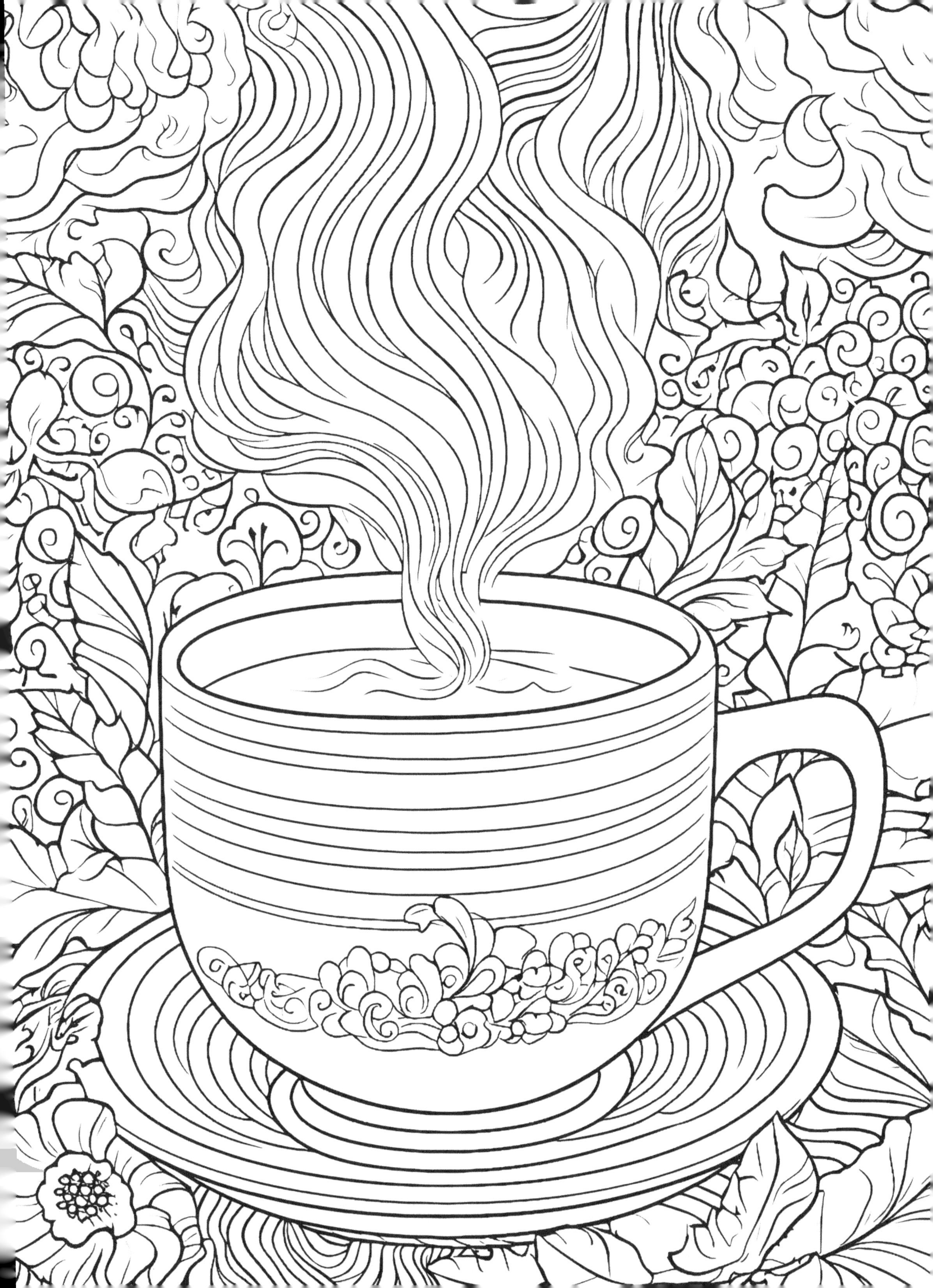

www.ingramcontent.com/pod-product-compliance
Lightning Source LLC
Chambersburg PA
CBHW082024230526
45466CB00023B/3354
* 9 7 9 8 3 9 3 4 9 0 6 9 0 *